POSTCARDS FROM THE GRAVE

Emir Suljagić

POSTCARDS FROM THE GRAVE

Afterword by
Ed Vulliamy

Translated by
Lejla Haverić

SAQI
in association with
The Bosnian Institute

British Library Cataloguing-in-Publication Date
A catalogue record of this book is available from the British Library

ISBN 0-86356-519-0
EAN 9-780863-565199

©Emir Suljagić
Translated for this edition by Lejla Haverić
Translation and edition © 2005 The Bosnian Institute (London)
Original manuscript title *Dopisnice iz groba*
Afterword © 2005 Ed Vulliamy

This edition first published 2005

Saqi Books
26 Westbourne Grove
London W2 5RH
www.saqibooks.com

in association with
The Bosnian Institute
14/16 St Marks Road
London W11 1RQ
www.bosnia.org.uk

Contents

Eastern Bosnia

Srebrenica Region

Glossary

APC	armoured personnel carrier
Bajram	Ottoman Muslim festival – Eid
Bašća, bašta	garden
B-H	Bosnia-Herzegovina
Blue Helmets	nickname for UNPROFOR troops
Chetniks	royalist irregulars in World War II, revived in post-communist Serbia – used as a generic term for Serb extremists
DMZ	demilitarized zone
Green Berets	militia organized by the SDA
JNA	Yugoslav People's Army [*Jugoslavenka Narodna Armija*]
Krmača [sow]	500 kg bomb
Maljutka [baby: Russian]	guided anti-tank missile
Osa [wasp]	type of portable rocket launcher
PTT	post, telegraph and telephone
Rakija	distilled spirit, often home-made
SDA	Party of Democratic Action [*Stranka Demokratske Akcije*] – Bosniak nationalist party led by Alija Izetbegović
SDS	Serb Democratic Party [*Srpska Demokratska Stranka*] – Serb nationalist party led by Radovan Karadžić
Stećak (plural *Stećci*]	Bosnian mediaeval tombstones
UNCIVPOL	United Nations Civilian Police
UNHCR	United Nations Military Observers
UNMO	United Nations High Commission for Refugees
UNPROFOR	United Nations Protection Force
VBR	multiple rocket launcher [*višećjevni bacač raketa*]
Vojvoda	'duke' – highest military title in royalist Yugoslavia, adopted by Chetniks and meaning roughly 'warlord'
White Eagles	Serbian paramilitaries organized by Vojislav Šešelj
Zolja [wasp][plural *zolje*]	type of portable rocket launcher

BOOK ONE

SURVIVING

I survived. My name could have been anything, Muhamed, Ibrahim or Isak, it does not matter. I survived and many did not; I lived on in the same way that they died. There is no difference between their death and my survival, for I remained to live in a world that has been permanently and irreversibly marked by their death. I come from Srebrenica. As a matter of fact, I come from somewhere else, but I chose to be from Srebrenica. Srebrenica is the only place I dare to come from and it was only to Srebrenica that I dared to set off, at a time when I dared to go nowhere else. That is the precise reason I believe that the place of birth is irrelevant compared to the place of death. The former does not say anything about us – it is a mere geographical fact; the place of death tells everything about our convictions, beliefs, the choices we made and stood by right until the end, until death caught up with us.

Maybe all of this is wrong, maybe you cannot choose your place of death after all, just like you cannot choose your place of birth. As for them, they died where they were born, where they sought and found refuge in the years of war, where they survived day after day in a shared agony. They chose Srebrenica in order to survive and this makes their death all the more terrible.

In mid May 1992, tens of thousands of people poured into Srebrenica, fleeing an onslaught by Serb forces. The artillery of the JNA was grinding down villages and towns and the dark smoke rising in the air ominously announced what was yet to come. Units of volunteers from Serbia were leaving a bloody trail behind them, sending the survivors ahead with blood-chilling stories. In the second week of May after thoroughly plundering it the Serbs

11

left Srebrenica, and it is on this town at the bottom of a steep and narrow valley that tens of thousands of desperate people converged. Among them were my friends, my acquaintances, my family and I.

I was to meet many people over the next three years, before the fall of the enclave formed in that summer of 1992. Some of them took the place of my cousins killed in 1992 or of Serb friends who had brutally betrayed me, and it was there that I experienced certain things for the first time in my life. But what we all had in common was a feeling of cosmic solitude, such as only those sentenced to death can feel. We observed each other, convinced that it was highly probable we would not see each other next day, and defeated by the feeling that this would not change anything.

Šaćir Begić was among the hundreds, probably thousands, of people I met. He was an old man whose strength of spirit kept surprising me time and again. Following some unwritten rule, nearly my whole neighbourhood would gather at his garden gate, discussing what they had heard on the radio that day, seen in the town, found out on the frontline ... In moments of common despair, when we all believed that it was the end – and such occasions were numerous during the three years of war – Šaćir, in his deep tobacco-scarred voice, would always conclude all our conversations by saying that 'everything will be much better than we expect'. When in July 1995 Serb forces finally – since it had been just a matter of time – overran the town, he too perished.

In death, or rather at the moment we cease to exist, there is no difference – gas chamber, mass execution or the treacherous flash of a metal blade in the dark, a painful sigh or rattle and the final stroke of the knife. Ten thousand people, ten thousand coffins, ten thousand gravestones – yeaaah, ten thousand! Everything is known about that death, or at least we now pretend that we want to know everything. We violate their death in newspaper columns, never asking ourselves questions about their life. We do not know anything about all those people who were not any less or more wonderful, good or bad than anyone else. Wonderful in so far as they were human. And in so far as I knew them.

When we got there, the town was deserted. We had been walking for most of the day, passing the Serb positions nearby, entrusting our lives to a teenage boy who claimed to know the way to the town. The rain that followed us all the way was of great help to us.

My mother and sister had stayed behind with some distant relatives in Skenderovići, one of the villages in a small pocket of territory near Srebrenica that had not yet been taken by the Serbs. The previous day we had heard on the radio that the town had been liberated and decided to try and get there, not knowing for sure if even that much was true.

Since 13 May we had been walking from one village to another, staying every night with different relatives we had never met before. It was only thanks to mother, whose family it was, that we had got quarters for the night. We had lost everything overnight as if we had woken up in some other world. No one had changed clothes for a week and mother, wearing father's outsize grey jacket, was clutching a blanket, the only thing she had managed to bring along from home. We did not know how much longer we could manage. A couple of days earlier I had found father hidden behind the house at which we had stayed that night, sitting against the wall and crying. He stopped crying and wiped his face with his hand, saying that grandfather had been killed, which later turned out to be just a rumour. But that moment forever changed our relationship.

It was his idea to set off for Srebrenica, and I think this illustrated quite well the extent of the despair into which he had sunk, along with all of us. The boy of my own age who was our guide, in a group containing another ten men and women, was the son of a friend of his and also our distant relative. I had only just started to discover that this was a community where we were all connected in some way.

One of the women walking behind us in the line was carrying a child born only a couple of months earlier. The child was crying the whole time and we were yelling at her, asking her to hush it up. She would blush and say that she could not, forgetting that we were getting closer to the Serb positions. As the guide warned us that we had reached the most dangerous stretch of the road, where Serb bunkers were some fifty metres away on both sides of the road, the child fell silent. And it stayed silent for nearly an hour, the time we needed to go past Pribićevac, the Serb village we feared most. When Nihad A. – that was the name of our guide – turned back to us from the head of the line to say that we were now safe, the child burst out crying so loudly that I felt it was making up for every second of silence. But now we did not mind its screaming, what is more we enjoyed it. That baby's cry was for us a sign of freedom, a sign that we were out of danger.

We found an abandoned town, grey and depressed, with streams of rain flowing down its steep streets. The houses in the centre had been burned down, their charred remains still fresh. The Serbs had left the town a day or possibly two days earlier, after Goran Zekić, president of the Srebrenica branch of SDS, had been killed. The simple and sole explanation I heard at that time was that Zekić had perished in an ambush, together with the young man who had killed him by throwing a bomb onto his car. This had become so commonplace in the war, I was ready to believe it. Supposedly the bomb was hand-made, like the ones I had often seen before: of simple manufacture, made with a couple of hundred grams of dynamite and packed with screws, nails and sharp fragments of metal that would be widely scattered by the explosion.

Serb sources always claimed that Hakija Meholjić's troops had killed Zekić as he was coming back from the funeral of some Serb soldier. However, in the next three years of war and after its end, a theory emerged according to which Zekić, a key figure in local SDS politics, in fact died as the result of a conflict with SDS hard-liners, as personified by Delivoje Sorak. The latter, who was commander of the Serb forces at Srebrenica, was in the car with him and survived the ambush. Following Zekić's death, he and another hard-liner Miodrag Jokić issued press statements full of contradictions, after which they were briefly held in custody but eventually released. It was a time when the enemy was clearly defined and any potential conflict within the Serb leadership had to be concealed.

Despite the fact that Meholjić's soldiers were at the time far away from the site of the murder, we all somehow believed in our explanation, because it meant that our forces were capable of causing serious damage to the Serbs. Serb sources had no interest in spreading a different story, so in the end both sides were happy to go along with that.

When we arrived, the town was still a kind of a no-man's land. In the town itself there was no one, just the odd inhabitant who had survived several weeks of terror. Pleased to see friendly faces, they told us how the Serbs, only the day before, had packed everything of any value onto trucks and left the town in panic.

They had driven in the direction of Skelani to the south of the town, then on to Serbia or along the left bank of Drina towards Bratunac. It was a far longer and less comfortable route, but the shorter and better one, which went to the north of the town through Potočari, was closed. In mid April a group of White Eagles – who were leading the attack on Bratunac – had been killed in an ambush on their way back from Srebrenica. The ambush was organised by Naser Orić, a former policeman from Srebrenica, and a group of poorly armed young men.

That was the first sign of resistance. Only a couple of months later, Srebrenica would become the first liberated town in Bosnia-Herzegovina. Or rather it was not liberated, since scarcely any battle was fought for it. The Serbs did not lose it but gave up on it, realising that although better armed they would not be able to defend it. And that narrow valley became the only place where we could seek refuge.

It was 18 May 1992. It was my first day in Srebrenica. I was to stay there for another three years, more than a thousand days that would all be identical to one another. But I remember that first day, it is different from all other days, it stands out from a long, monotonous succession of days, probably only because it was the first.

What I remember it for is the rain, a cold spring rain and spring was late that year; for large raindrops beating on our shoulders and backs, penetrating our wet clothes. I also remember it for a grey sky that looked ominous, though back then we could have not known why that was so. I remember it as probably the only day in my life when I felt complete freedom, strange as that may sound, given that the town was encircled by the Serbs. The day when for the first time I felt – and it was all I felt – a deep inner drive to survive.

***

Only a month earlier, I had been hiding together with my father and a couple of neighbours in the woods on the hill above Voljavica, a village near Bratunac where I lived with my family. Fearfully we watched cars passing by below in the valley, their sirens wailing. The sound of sirens was frightening, but even more terrifying was the fact that they belonged to the White Eagles, a paramilitary group connected to Vojislav Šešelj and the Serbian Radical Party. They had arrived in Bratunac a couple of days before and with the help of the JNA and local Serbs taken over the town.

On that same day, all Bosniak policemen had handed over their weapons. A couple of days later the Križevica, a river that flows through Bratunac and into the Drina, started to wash ashore sporadically the corpses of prominent Bosniaks. The roads between the town and its nearby villages were cut, the phone lines disconnected. That was the signal for us to leave our houses and hide in the woods above the village.

One of our neighbours drove a car into the woods, thus demonstrating not only his impressive driving skills but also the insanity that had affected him along with us all. It was a *Zastava 101*, thanks to which we were at least able to listen to the news from a weak radio set.

The rest of the country was already at war and we sat there for days on end, confused and scared, without much talking. Everyone was concerned about his own future. Some went back to the village at night to sleep at home, as if by doing so they sought to deny the reality of what was happening to us. At dawn they would return to the woods, stupidly and naively believing we were safer up there.

On the day of 12 May 1992 when Radio Bosnia-Herzegovina announced that Lieutenant-General Ratko Mladić had been nominated commander of JNA troops in the country (or more precisely commander of the Second Military District of the JNA), Muslim villages around Bratunac started being set on fire. It was a coincidence – such a widespread persecution of the population must have been planned much earlier – but it was a coincidence that did not augur well. We had been hiding for two weeks already, since mid April, and were by now well into May without knowing what was to come. That day all our doubts were set at rest.

News from the cut off and occupied town were brought to us by Ibro S., a boy nicknamed *Žućo* [yellowy] because of his yellow-ginger hair and the countless freckles of the same colour on his face. He was fifteen or sixteen years old, but because of his size no one would have thought him older than twelve. People were getting increasingly nervous without cigarettes, so they gave him small bundles of worthless Yugoslav money to go to town and fetch them some. They were not able or did not dare to do it themselves. The road was swarming with Serb barricades, but Žućo rode past them on a bicycle so big that his feet could scarcely reach the pedals, and he always came back with the red packs of *Filter Jugoslavija*.

Along with cigarettes he brought information, relating whereabouts he had seen each of our Serb neighbours, now wearing camouflage uniforms and carrying machine guns. He was the first to tell us, to our horror, that the Serbs were gathering men from nearby villages in the basement of the Vuk Karadžić primary school. Terrified, I heard how a certain Idriz had been killed, a man I knew only as the driver of my school bus. Serb soldiers had put him against a wall and repeatedly driven the bus into him until he died.

That day, when Ibro returned from town, he told us how he had

17

been let through the barricade by Ranko Obrenović, a house-painter from a neighbouring village who had lost his left hand while playing with a bomb found a couple of years after the Second World War. I knew that story, I had heard it before from his son Aleksandar Obrenović, my best friend from school. I had been to his house countless times, I had shared a school desk with him for eight years. His father was now manning a barricade, one-armed, clumsy as he must have looked with a rifle. And my memories flooded back.

During my last year of primary school, as Slobodan Milošević's 'anti-bureaucratic revolution' was well underway, as the leaderships in Montenegro, Vojvodina and Kosovo were removed and tension grew in other parts of the former Yugoslavia, I witnessed the impact those events had on everyday life. A boy from my class – actually the child of a mixed marriage, which is probably not irrelevant to this story – cursed my 'Turkish mother' during a lesson. I realised then for the first time that, for reasons beyond my understanding, I was somehow different from some of my schoolmates.

Of course, I waited for him after class. I was deeply hurt and wanted to return the insult with interest. Aleksandar joined me as a partisan observer. We knocked him down and started kicking him. As he rolled about in pain, Aleksandar kept kicking him and saying through clenched teeth: 'Fuck your Chetnik mother'. He, a boy carrying the name of the heir to the Serbian throne assassinated in 1902, defended my 'Turkish honour' back then. A couple of years later his father stood armed at a barricade.

Later, during the war, I asked around to find out what had happened to him. I found out that he had remained exactly as I knew him – a rascal who on guard duty would throw ammunition boxes into fire, then laugh at his sleepy, dazed comrades as they ran from the trenches like mad things. I did not ask whether he remembered how he had once defended a 'Turk'.

Soon after Ibro told us about what he had seen and heard in town, thick pillars of light-coloured smoke started rising from villages on the hills around the town. We watched, for the first time we watched with our own eyes how other people's houses burn, just as we would later see our own houses burning. And we did not want to believe it. Or rather we did not dare to believe it, because it meant that a point of no return had been reached. On the right – the Serbian – bank of the Drina, a long column of big trucks covered in white tarpaulins grew steadily longer. We counted up to thirty of them and then gave up as the trucks headed towards Bratunac. While the villages burned, Serb soldiers chased the population out of the hills down to the main road where, in an incredibly synchronised operation, trucks waited for them in a line whose end was still in Serbia.

That night my father woke me up and whispered to me to get dressed quickly. Still half asleep, I obeyed and got dressed in the dark, hurrying to leave the house and join him outside where he was waiting impatiently. With him walking in front of me we set off, I did not know where to. After nearly an hour's trudge through the woods, we got to a clearing where a couple of hundred men had already gathered. It was way after midnight and the hubbub on the meadow rose as dawn broke. A fairly big group of people, some of them armed, separated and continued on further towards villages deep in the hills. The largest group stayed put on the meadow wondering what to do.

Father and I left at dawn. With us was Juso C., our cousin and neighbour, who had been to Podloznik several times. This was a village on the border between the two municipalities of Bratunac and Srebrenica that was difficult for Serb APCs to reach. The expelled population from the Drina valley was already gathering there. Dawn had broken when, after continuous climbing, we got to a clearing below which a road meandered. We had to cross the road: there were no Serbs on the other side and we would be safe there, as safe as was possible. To the left was a magnificent view of the Drina, which stretched through green fields. The dew that had built up on my shoes was coming through, making my toes wet, and I was cold. But I could not take my eyes off the river, more beautiful than ever in those seventeen years that I had spent growing up on its banks. It was all the more beautiful because I knewI should never again swim in its rapids, never again dive into it at the risk of breaking my neck.

After about an hour and a half of walking towards the southwest we reached the road. A car drove by below us. This was the moment that we had to run across the road and then climb up the hill on the other side, before the car returned or someone else turned up. At one point we heard the sound of an engine behind our backs, so we ducked down in the high grass, without knowing if the people in the car had spotted us. When the noise faded, we got up again and continued our route to Podloznik.

***

Tired from the journey, I fell asleep curled up in the doorway, on the front step of a house belonging to one of the many of our cousins I was to meet. I woke up in a bed where my father had probably carried me. A complete stranger lay next to me, fully dressed like myself, a man I had never seen before. But my father was not in the room. I got up and started looking for him in the overcrowded house. He was outside with my mother and sister, who had arrived the previous night in a group of several hundred women and children. Mother told us that all the other relatives, nearly the whole neighbourhood, had surrendered to the new Serb authorities who had guaranteed them safety and free passage to Tuzla. What is more Granny, father's mother, had been to look for us the day before in our hideout in the woods, in order to try and persuade us to surrender. Three months later we found out that all our relatives who had surrendered had been executed by firing squad. The elderly who obeyed the authorities' order to stay in the village and look after the cattle were collected into a house, killed and then burnt.

From there we went on to another village, Storesko. Mother knew of another distant relative there, with whom we could stay for a night. I do not know how long we stayed there. But in that village and some neighbouring ones the first groups were already being organised to stand up against what was brazenly called the Serb Territorial Defence. Wanting to demonstrate their seriousness, those groups decided to attack the Serb positions overlooking and controlling the road from Bratunac to the lead mine in Sase.

The attack was doomed to fail from the start and in fact ended in total fiasco. Poorly armed, the men had no chance of victory. But the failure was eventually blamed on a young man who, after crawling silently with a grenade in his hand to within ten metres of a Serb trench, was seized with a coughing fit, thus exposing himself and all the others. At least there were no fatalities. In the meantime, Mother remembered we had yet another cousin in Skenderovići and father heard on the radio the news that Srebrenica was free. The next day we set off for the town, the first of many thousands who were to follow our example.

***

None of my companions on that journey is alive. Juso, with whom I left home, died in July 1995 near free territory, in a group that was trying to get through from Srebrenica to Tuzla on foot. Nihad, who brought me to Srebrenica, did not survive July 1995. My father returned home and died in his garden in December 1992.

The following notes are the result of about ten conversations with a relative of mine who was imprisoned in the camp in Sušica, near Vlasenica. His family, who incidentally lived in my neighbourhood, was arrested; he and his father were imprisoned, his mother and sister were deported to Kladanj. His father was later murdered. After his imprisonment in the camp, he was released and arrived in Srebrenica in late summer 1992. He was one of the first people who got through to the territory controlled by government forces after the fall of Srebrenica in July 1995. Today he lives in the USA and has asked to remain anonymous.

I do not know exactly how much time I spent in the camp. I was imprisoned at the end of May and set free in mid June. 'Drive them to Cerska, let them starve to death', said a soldier who stopped our bus on its way to Kladanj. The driver made a U-turn without a word. He apologised for not being able to drive us any further. We had to walk about 10 km to our frontlines in Cerska.

* * *

The first person I met on my arrival in the camp was the camp governor Dragan Nikolić – 'Jenki'. He came in through the door and suddenly all the prisoners pulled back. They all pressed together in a corner, as if they wanted to be as tiny and invisible as possible so as to avoid being noticed or sticking out in any way that would attract his attention. As he opened the door I happened to find myself between him and a prisoner.
  – 'Where are you going?'
  – 'To the toilet.'

Slap! I did not even see the punch coming, I just fell over; stars shot through my head.

– 'Get back there!'

I saw him later, he came back two or three times a day and took girls out. They generally did not come back. Nor did the men. Someone called Lukić would take them out. He would stand in front of us and observe carefully. He would then point to someone: 'You!' They would then slowly shuffle to the exit, knowing they had been sentenced to death.

* * *

We were beaten every day. I was then only seventeen years old but I was covered in bruises. During the first fifteen days of imprisonment, before I got to Sušica, I had not eaten anything. I had sometimes managed to get the prison guards in Vlasenica to let me go to the toilet, where I took a drink of water. I had already lost 20 kg and could barely stand up. On the first day in Sušica, a woman who had just arrived from one of the recently cleansed villages close to Vlasenica gave me some bread. I ate half a kilo straight away and then fainted. My body could not cope with that much food at a time. I had not been to the toilet for about twenty days, and since leaving the hangar could be fatal I was reluctant to ask. We never left the hangar and if we went outside for one moment we were beaten.

* * *

We were beaten at other times too – with metal-pointed sticks, wire cable, baseball bats. They would stick a rifle into someone's mouth. I watched how a guard stuck a sniper rifle in a man's mouth. The barrel of a sniper rifle is longer than any other and the man had swallowed nearly the whole of it. Sometimes I lost my voice singing Chetnik songs. On one occasion I remember chanting 'King-dom of Ser-bia' for more than two hours. During that time in Sušica I could not get to sleep. In fact sleep was impossible: guards would constantly enter the hangar and randomly beat the people who were piled on top of each other in the dark.

* * *

I was captured in mid May at home together with my father. They promised that they would not do us any harm. What is more they said: 'Nothing will happen to your family!' Two weeks later a bus with police escort arrived in our part of town. They asked us to take only what was essential and hurry onto the bus – we were being taken to Kladanj. But in Nova Kasaba we encountered a checkpoint. The soldier who got onto the bus ordered all the men to get out. The bus then left. We stood in the meadow and stared at the bus taking away our families, mothers, sisters. Three days later they drove us again from Vlasenica to Kasaba. There were thirty-eight of us, chosen to be shot. They lined us up on a meadow facing twelve soldiers and an APC. Behind a big machine-gun I recognised Željko Lukić, a bus driver who drove the very bus I used to take to school every day. It is a lie that people facing death do not see their whole life passing before their eyes. I saw my whole life in one minute. A soldier stepped out of the firing squad. He came up to me:

– 'When were you born?'

– '1975.'

– 'What are you doing here?'

I grabbed my father's hand and said 'I am here with my father, I don't want to leave him'.

'Come on, get lost, this isn't a place for you!' he said. He then made me step out of the line along with four other boys of my age and took us to a spot from which we could not see the execution site. We were walking when we heard the firing behind our backs. I turned round and I swear – maybe I only imagined it – but I do swear I saw my father fall.

Enclave. This cold and precise word denotes all the differences between us, inside, and them outside. We never called Srebrenica an 'enclave', because that had absolutely nothing to do with our reality. We called it cauldron, world's end, appendix, probably because those words better described how we felt. What we were going through every day was inaccessible to the rest of the world.

After the war I looked up a definition of the word enclave in a dictionary of foreign words. This is what I found: an outlying portion of a country surrounded by the territory of another country; ethnic or any other community separated from its greater part; land property surrounded on all sides by the property of another owner.

The reality of a small town under a three-year siege is much more akin to a ghetto or a concentration camp. True, comparison with a ghetto is not correct either. You could sometimes leave the ghetto, at least in the beginning; it was possible to move freely even outside the walls. In the enclave there were no barbed wire, watch towers, armed guards and dogs, gas chambers, as in concentration camps. Its border shifted constantly, it was neither permanent nor stable, and the fact that it kept moving to the advantage of the stronger party was terrifying. The danger was not as visible as in a camp where it is personified by a sullen guard in uniform. On the contrary, it was people we could not see who decided who was going to live, not wanting to know who their victims were, not seeing the agonised expressions on their faces, not giving them a chance to prepare.

The Serb guns were too far away to be seen from the town, but close enough for us to be scared of them. Close enough to be conscious every moment – whether we were in bed, eating, sitting, walking, laughing or talking – of the noise rending the air and of the death those guns brought faster than the speed of thought. It was not like in Sarajevo for instance, which was shelled for hours every day. On the contrary, here shells rent the sky and fell according to their own rhythm, when and where they wanted, as if they had acquired personal habits, minds and plans independent of the Serb gunners and their barrels.

Most lives were lost precisely because shells were unexpected, because people were not used to accepting or refused to accept the fact that shells had become part of our lives. In one little square in the town, stuck – or rather nailed by shrapnel – to the walls of a nearby building and kiosk were the remains of a woman killed in the first months of war, as she walked home from the market carrying her meagre purchases. Thousands of people crossed the square every day and nobody paid any attention to the parts of her body that had in the meantime rotted. It was easier for us to get used to death than to what had caused it. Death was acceptable but fear of death was not.

We used to kill the time before and after our only meal, or between two daily meals, in a little park between the department store and the town café, between those two textbook examples of socialist-realist architecture and two invariable features of every Bosnian provincial town. We sat on a cold concrete wall or the short flight of steps leading to park benches washed by rain and bleached by the sun. We watched the broad street. In front of our scared, boyish eyes a world was falling apart and from its ugly remains a new one was emerging.

We were watching in order to get slowly used to it, to accept it as the only possible reality, until we forgot that beyond our surroundings there was another world. We stopped tormenting ourselves with questions about it, even forgetting that we used to have different lives. Together we progressively forgot what we were missing out on, forgot everything that was happening behind the walls erected around us. And we were so good at it that we eventually started despising the outside world. We lived in an impermanent world and mocked the longevity of the one outside. It looked trivial to us, because we had learnt that longevity does not necessarily bring experience.

People were stunned by the fact that they had become so worthless overnight and found this difficult to accept. Those people did not understand that their survival depended on how quickly they grasped that it was not possible to bring anything from the old world into the new. The old world was irreversibly lost and the new one was ruled by scum, criminals, former prisoners, corrupt policemen ...

We would meet up there every day. Mujo Džananović and I had both been late for the first class on the first day of the first year of secondary school. We had met as we were waiting for the class to finish, and for the pupil in charge to open the doors, which had to stay shut after the first bell. For the next three years we had always sat at the same school desk, second from the door. We both looked older than we were. He had started shaving early and his face was covered in heavy black stubble. It was only thanks to the lack of weapons that we were not on the front line.

As if by some tacit agreement we always arrived at the park at the same time, after failing in an attempt to cheat hunger by frantically reading or sleeping. We were at that fragile and transitory age when we were still discovering ourselves and revealing ourselves to others. At that age we form our first opinions, the first feelings start budding within us, and the world becomes more sensual than hitherto.

Mujo was the taciturn type, he never said much. I do not know if I have ever seen him angry and his attempts at being angry generally made me laugh. When I think about it, I realise that I never knew him that well, despite the fact that we shared – or at least I thought we did – nearly everything during three years of school and three years of war. Unlike most of our friends, neither he nor I sought comfort in acrid home-made *rakija* that burnt the stomach and destroyed the brain. At least not at that time.

Later on I started drinking with the others, but I soon realised we were all too young ever to get used to *rakija*. But that made me drink it all the harder.

Some smoked their first cigarettes. They would slowly roll the tobacco that crumbled into dust in small plastic bags and got stuck to lips, dappled with dark stains. More was spilled than put onto the paper. The cigarette would then go round. They would count the drags that each of them took and argue about the 'roach', the end of the cigarette that burned the fingers. I was popular because at that time I still did not smoke.

We learned fast. Our upbringing and our intelligence, our values were not worth a row of beans. So we had started to content ourselves with scraps, since we could get nothing else, while staying true to ourselves and not losing our identities.

After the war, Mujo's mother lived close to my house in Sarajevo for a long time. Every time my mother ran into her on the street, she came home in tears, telling me over and over again that I should visit Mujo's mother. I could never bring myself to do that, because I knewI should feel guilty in her presence. After all, Mujo and I were the same andI should not be able to explain, above all to myself, what gave me the right to come out alive from that school desk, second from the door, when he did not. We had had the same doubts, the same desires, the same fears and also the same rare things that used to make us happy then. And nevertheless it was me who escaped.

He perished in something that we expected – understanding that it would take a long time before even that world in which we found ourselves came to an end, vanished in an explosion; and at the same time being afraid, because we did not know if we would survive yet another big bang. The worst thing about his death is that it happened years after we accepted leading a semi-existence, accepted that we would never be exceptional or what we were once destined to be, because that was the only way to make sure we would carry on living.

The Serbs around the enclave were the masters of our future. We were taken way back into the past and we knew that the future was not ours, that even if we survived we would live lives which had nothing in common with us. We were growing up in torn jumpers, stolen shoes, trousers acquired from the plunder of a village not yet burnt down. We lived on borrowed time, gnawed by rotten teeth, off charity bread … and all of it in vain. We were equally irrelevant to everyone.

In the years to come, I got to know the internal mechanics of the town authorities very well, and came to understand how much they had contributed to our general hopelessness and despair.

What I always found striking was the coarseness of those people, who until then had been anonymous, and the simplicity with which their clearly divided world functioned. All I could make out was that in the first weeks of war, in a village near Srebrenica, they had split the tasks up among themselves according to some sort of tribal principle. Each person in power in one way or another represented one of the 'warlords' in the enclave. But each of them had their own understanding of power. From the very beginning of the war right up until its tragic fall, the enclave was under a sort of internal siege, or at least that is what it felt like to me.

I had experienced the tribal nature of that power on my own skin, at the beginning of winter 1993. It was a time when humanitarian aid was being dropped to us from the air. One night in February 1993, my uncle was one of the thousands of people who were waiting on the hills around the town.

He was killed, before a crowd of onlookers, as he ran towards the palettes that were landing in the vicinity. His wife and two children were waiting for him at home. The murderer, who opened fire on the pretext that my uncle had crossed his field looking for food, was related to the president of the municipality. There was no police enquiry. That man was never executed, or even convicted of murder, in what was their usual display of untouchability. My aunt and her two children were soon evacuated from the town and never tried to raise the issue, even when they got to Tuzla.

For three years I saw the people who had prevented the investigation of my uncle's murder almost every day. As a matter of fact, I met the man who had committed the crime and understood how it could have happened. During those three years before Srebrenica fell, we returned to a primitive form of community. There were no laws and public authority was based on a mutual balance of power. Every time I saw that man it made my stomach churn, but I never dared to mention the murder, since I knew that it would not change anything. There is no point in naming him today either.

I saw them every day and became aware of growing differences between them and the population of the enclave. It was impossible to tell when exactly power had become an end in itself for them, but over time the gap widened and deepened. I felt sick seeing the president of the municipal council show off with his stiff cardboard packs of *Marlboro* bought from Canadian or Dutch soldiers, while my friends continued to make cigarettes out of bad paper and bitter home-grown tobacco that pinched the throat and burned into black ashes. Some municipal-council officials had the insolence to drive round in cars, whereas ordinary people had to walk dozens of kilometres wearing bad shoes. Even at times of famine their tables were groaning with food, whereas my granny only had soya to cook.

It just makes Mujo's death and the deaths of other dear ones that much harder for me to bear. After that, nothing had sense anymore. Not life, let alone death.

By July 1992, hunger had become the central factor in the life of every inhabitant of the enclave. We had one, rarely two, meals a day. The town was full of exhausted people who spent their days wandering aimlessly around. Or they rested, hiding deep in the cool shade of their flats. In the early evening small groups of people stood in front of buildings and discussed, rather too loudly, what they had heard on the news.

The hungrier and more exhausted they were, the louder their discussions. The more hopeless they were, the more heated the arguing would get, as if they wanted to compensate for the general feeling of powerlessness. They then returned to their homes to spend yet another long night, the silence of which would be broken by a sudden artillery attack, or by hunger so gnawing that no dream, no matter how deep, could offer resistance.

Breakfast, lunch and supper were the privilege of the few, of people who were close to the warlords and the new caste of war profiteers, who had already started to emerge in the town. The regime of hunger inflicted upon the ordinary people consisted of one meal a day, generally at noon and never big enough to appease that hunger.

We were sticking to the habit of calling it lunch, refusing to yield to new circumstances, as if we wanted to hang on to what our recent lives had been, even if only through the language we used. The second meal was generally taken late at night, as late as possible. We would swallow a couple of mouthfuls, if we had that much. And still we got up in the morning hungrier than the night before and even more exhausted than on the morning before.

In summer the days got longer, too long, and sunset was not a call to supper. The most difficult time was the afternoon. Hunger would then turn into a pain, similar to a stomach cramp, a pain that could not be banished. In Sarajevo after the war I met a young man from Foča who had spent the war in Goražde, which had also been besieged for three years. Together we calculated quite accurately that during those years we had got fewer calories per day than the prisoners in Stalin's gulags.

Everyone pretended not to notice that each day the others looked thinner than the previous day. They became darker, their faces were losing their natural colour, and everyone simply started to look like everyone else, bloodless and almost featureless. In the end, they all did become the same: the same grey wrinkled skin, the dark circles round the eyes, the tired gaze. But talking about food was below our dignity. Thin soup and sometimes the last reserves of beans were on the menu. After that there was nothing left.

While the refugees in town were starving, the peasants from the villages around Srebrenica were more or less spared. They continued working their fields, not paying attention to the poor and hungry newcomers who overnight had lost everything they had worked for all their lives. They sometimes even commented: 'Why didn't you defend yourselves?' When the hunger became unbearable, and those worst affected started taking family jewels and the last Deutschmarks saved long ago out of well-hidden bundles in order to buy food, the peasants used the opportunity to make money.

'I gave away my wedding ring for a couple of kilos of peppers', one elderly acquaintance told me. He was not the only one to give away the last of his possessions for a little bit of flour, a couple of eggs or a tiny bit of cheese. There were legions like him who wandered through the villages, some of them begging, some trading the last remnants of their lives. Soon a monstrous market was set up in which people mostly traded goods for goods, because almost no one believed in money any more.

Tradesmen exchanged cigarettes and matches from the remains of their pre-war stocks for potatoes or flour. That summer, for one box of matches one could get 10 kg of potatoes or ten eggs, sometimes a kilo of cheese. On one occasion I sold matches in nearby villages for one of the town tradesmen, in exchange for a commission. Walking from one village to another I noticed that hunger had completely altered my personality. From a boy who before the war used to be shy and reserved, I had become aggressive and cruel. From a seventeen-year-old who used to freeze in front of the girls in my class, I had become aggressive and unscrupulous. What I saw scared me, but I quickly realised that it was a matter of survival.

– 'Do you want to buy matches?'
– 'How much are they?'
– 'One box for ten kilos of potatoes.'
– 'That's expensive.'
– What do you mean, expensive? You've got ten tons in your field and you can't spare ten kilos! But what do I care, you're the one who'll be sitting in the dark.

This I once said to a peasant who was digging potatoes out of the ground. An hour later I took the same road back, struggling to carry a sack of potatoes I had got from someone else. The peasant saw me from far away, came onto the road and said he would buy a box of matches for 10 kg of potatoes.

– 'It's more expensive now – fifteen', I said.
– 'That's way over the top.'
– 'All right, twelve and not a gram less.'
– 'OK,' said the farmer and told his wife to put roughly 12 kg into the bag.
– 'Not roughly,' I said and triumphantly pulled out a small set of scales.

After we had used up all the stocks of white flour, we switched to wholemeal and then to maize flour. Next came oats, which were impossible to grind well enough, so not only was the flour bitter, but it also hurt our sore throats. Stalks and hazel bushes were also ground up in water mills.

When in March 1993 General Philippe Morillon arrived in Srebrenica, he was offered a slice of hazel-bush bread so that he could see for himself what the inhabitants of Srebrenica were surviving off. After he had tasted the bread, he said, a little embarrassed, that it was 'healthy, good for the digestion'.

The months passed slowly, but the town market was as busy and noisy as before the war. The fact that they could not do anything with their earnings did not bother the tradesmen at all. After my short experiment of selling matches, I never again got a chance to test the strength of my character. Today I am glad I did not, because I do not dare to think whatI should have turned into. But all that time we were sinking lower and lower, and when winter arrived there was nothing we would not have done for a piece of bread.

The scale of values for the most important trading articles in the town was most brutally dictated by the war, by the balance of forces on the front. By March 1993 the Serbs were advancing on the borders of the enclave, and people from nearby villages started to arrive in the town, carrying everything they owned or had had time to bring along. They arrived carrying bundles over their shoulders or with clothes hastily piled onto horse-drawn carts. They brought along cattle, which were of little use to them.

They had lost their land and their crops, and the cattle they brought with them had to be slaughtered after a couple of days and exchanged for corn on the town market. In the first days the exchange rate was one to one, but with each Serb attack and each torched Bosniak village the price of meat went down. After a couple of weeks one kilo of corn was worth three or four kilos of meat.

It was hard to watch them arriving in town, on horse– or bullock-drawn carts, with families, with children more or less carefully wrapped in rugs supposed to protect them from the cold. Some people felt for them, whereas others thought they had got what they deserved. But their arrival meant that danger was getting closer too, so that even the latter had no time to gloat.

I had been working for UNMO (United Nations Military Observers) for a couple of weeks, maybe even months, when a Danish policeman, whose name I cannot recall, asked me to translate a daily report that they (in this case the United Nations Civilian Police) were getting from the Srebrenica police station.

As UNCIVPOL did not have an interpreter of their own, it had become normal that interpreters from other UN agencies occasionally worked for them too. After I had translated the report, he pulled out a pack of cigarettes as a token of gratitude – it was *Kim Menthol* I remember – from the big trunk he kept in his room and handed it to me. I was confused because I was not used to being paid – I had previously been working for three meals a day and that made me feel privileged. I asked him in all sincerity: 'What shall I do with it?' The fact that I did not even smoke at that time made me all the more confused.

He coldly replied: 'Sell them, then' and left the pack on the wooden counter in the post-office hall. I looked at those cigarettes, debating what to do with them. I could have sold them, but did not want to; a second option was to give them to someone, but I knew that they would still end up on the black market. The third option was to smoke them. This is what I did, knowing that even though I might damage my health, at least my honour would still be intact.

By the end of winter 1992, the price of a pack of cigarettes reached the incredible sum of 150, even 200 Deutschmarks. A pack of cigarettes mostly meant a miraculously saved packet of Sarajevo-manufactured *Drina* 'white brand'. Before the Serb offensive, the only other source of cigarettes that I knew of, thanks to a cousin of mine who bought and sold cigarettes for one of Naser Orić's aides, was a tradesman from Gostilj, a village on the road between Srebrenica and Potočari. As a middleman, my cousin had to go over to the man's house under shellfire. He generally waited until dark to undertake the trip. He would come back late at night or the next morning with a couple of packs that he then sold on the market. He took the money to the man he worked for, but made sure that there was at least a packet or two left for him.

Those without money racked their brains how to get hold of tobacco. Some sowed it in plant pots during the summer and kept it on their balconies. Every morning they carefully picked leaves from the bottom upwards, dried them on a cooking stove and then crumbled the dry but still green leaves onto the page of a newspaper. Those who could not afford even this smoked quince– or apple-tree leaves, coltsfoot leaves, the leaves of nettles, plantains or any plant at all.

With the arrival of UN forces, cigarettes got cheaper. Even by the first week the price had dropped to 50 Marks a packet and then gradually went down to 10 or 15 Marks depending on the brand. Canadian and later Dutch soldiers bought cigarettes in their canteen for 2 Marks, sold them to black marketeers for 5, and the latter would then resell them for two or three times as much to the few citizens of Srebrenica who could afford it.

As long as the Canadian soldiers were in town, the market was saturated with *Players*, the most popular brand amongst them. The most prestigious and expensive brand was *Marlboro*, obtainable from UN soldiers. Soon cigarettes were also obtainable from the other side of the front. *LM* arrived from Žepa, where opportunistic Ukrainian soldiers deployed in that enclave resold cigarettes. Black marketeers bought *VEK*, *Bond* or the almost forgotten and tasteless *Partner* direct from Serbs at a checkpoint known as the Yellow Bridge.

In the next two years cigarettes became one of the things around which people's lives revolved. No matter how many cigarettes there were in the enclave, there were never enough. They became one of the two or three solid currencies. You could pay and get paid in cigarettes, buy and sell for cigarettes. I remember with disgust how a Jordanian soldier, who had arrived in Srebrenica in the summer of 1993, once came up to me and quietly asked under his breath if I could get him a girl; he would pay in cigarettes, he said.

I told him that I could not help him, that I did not know anything about it. But he managed without my help. A girl was found for him by one of the older boys who, from the moment the UN entered the town, spent literally every moment in front of the PTT building. I do not know how much he paid, but I do know that he did not stop there. He was buying all sorts of things. My stomach turned as I watched him taking a huge golden ring, possibly the biggest I had ever seen, from an elderly man in exchange for three packets of cigarettes. I knew he was not the only one, but unlike some of my colleagues I did not want to take part in it.

Actually there was one time when I did break the promise I had made to myself. One day a cousin of mine, who had started trafficking in cigarettes after he was left alone in the town, came to see me at work. The guard called for me and I went to the entrance. He was visibly anxious. He told me that he owed money to someone, about 200 Marks, and that he would at the very least get beaten unconscious by someone I dreaded even to think of. A carton of cigarettes would pay off his debt, but he could not afford it.

'OK', I said, 'You'll get a carton of cigarettes. But only this once'. 'And five or six kilos of sugar', he added. I did not know what he needed sugar for, but I promisedI should get that too. A couple of days later one of the observers went to Bratunac for negotiations. He got back with a carton of *Partner* and five kilos of sugar. That night it was easier for me to fall asleep, even if on the previous days I had been tormented by the fact that I had violated the only principle one could believe in those days, namely that one should not make profit out of other people's sorrow.

'We're off to gather food', people used to say in the first year of war, meaning by that the long journey from Srebrenica to the villages in the Drina valley, to unplundered farms and cellars to look for any remaining bits of food. Every night several thousands of people would gather in Podloznik, after they had walked dozens of kilometres from town, mainly on forest paths. Protected by the darkness, they would then set off on an uncertain journey.

The road went literally between Serb bunkers and thousands of people could not pass unnoticed. Whole families went on those journeys: fathers took their sons, husbands took their wives, hoping that they would survive and carry enough food back to make it last and spare them another similar trip. Still, many people were trapped forever in the Serb ambushes that became more and more frequent as time went on, taking an ever heavier toll.

The Serbs generally let them reach their destination, then waited on the demarcation line to catch them on their way back, exhausted both from the journey and the load they were carrying. Sufficiently close for the firing to be heard in nearby villages, but too far for Bosnian soldiers in the vicinity to be able or dare to help them. During the night, under the deafening noise of guns, rocket launchers and *Zolje*, one could hear the final screams of the desperate and starving people. Generally there were no soldiers among them. They were mostly unarmed civilians, women, and sometimes even children. Only a few of them carried a gun or a hand grenade, just in case they 'fell into the hands' of the Serbs, which was considered worse than death.

For a long time a story circulated about Sead M., a young man

I knew from before the war because his house was right next to the school bus stop. The Serbs captured him and then allegedly paraded him around Bratunac as a trophy, drugged and with a big cross hanging on his chest. Occasionally they would drive him to the demarcation line to show him to the soldiers in the trenches on the other side. It is true that Sead was captured during one of the food-gathering trips. But it is not known whether like most people he got killed straight away, or if such a cruel fate had indeed befallen him. I doubted this story back then just as much as I do today. But along with every new detail it acquired each time it was retold among the population of the enclave, this story was the best illustration in the popular imagination of the degree of cruelty that those who thought of surrendering could expect. Entire families vanished on those journeys.

My neighbour Šećo Mašić and his wife both got killed, leaving behind two children – one a little over a year old, the other born right at the start of the war.

That longer route was used until July 1992 when forces from Srebrenica took control of Zalazje, a village to the northeast of the town. The village, consisting of a mere sprinkling of houses between two hills, was turned into a military stronghold. It was situated on a considerably shorter route from Srebrenica to the villages that represented a source of food. The new, shorter road had its good points: people could set off and come back in one night instead of two. They were able to carry more and do the trip several times in one night.

It was nevertheless a tough journey. It was 15 km in one direction, through unfriendly regions that had been given a wide berth even before. People would come back to the territory of Srebrenica tired, sweaty and with almost 10 km still ahead of them. The heaviest load anyone ever carried was 62 kg of corn. Hajrudin S., my close relative whose wife had given birth to a daughter a couple of weeks earlier, brought a sack on his back strapped on with cords that left marks ingrained in his shoulders. To friends who asked him why he was inflicting that upon himself, given that it was not the first time he had carried back more than 50 kg, he replied: 'I need to get milk for the child. And a litre costs two kilos – of corn'.

After several new ambushes and new fatalities, the civilians finally got a military escort that cleared the mines off the road and offered a minimum of protection while they hurriedly gathered food. In return they gave the soldiers part of their pickings. This lasted until the winter of that year, when nearly the whole region had been liberated. But it was too late: almost all the stocks of food had given out, cellars had been emptied, and crops from the previous spring had gone rotten. From then on we had to go and get food from Serb villages, which meant new battles, new unnecessary fatalities. But that yellow corn was not just food, it was a currency with which one could buy life.

Early every morning before the fog above the narrow valley of Srebrenica dispersed, literally hundreds of people would climb the hills around the town. Dressed in the dirty rags they had worn the previous morning and stinking of dried sweat, each would be carrying an axe and a rope. Their destination was the woods, and it was sometimes necessary literally to clamber on hands and knees to get through to the top of the cliffs and reach a small, bleak plain.

They did not go deep into the woods. In order to save energy, they knocked down the first tree they saw, then tied a rope round it and dragged it several hundred metres. The tree would turn and get stuck in the bushes, its sharp top driving into the ground, so that it was with great pleasure that they would finally push it off the cliff. Following goat tracks they would descend slowly in pursuit of it. There at the bottom they would drag the tree home through the town.

On one such morning, as I was absorbed in blowing onto fresh cuts left by the rope on the palms of my hands, a tree trunk rolled down to the base of the hill, hitting the wall of the house where I lived with a dull thud. Suddenly the skies opened. I was sure of that.

The explosion was so powerful that I became genuinely concerned that something inside me might have burst. My ears were ringing and in panic I started running down the hill. I was not watching my steps, instantly forgetting that I could break my neck if I stepped a millimetre off the path or trod on a stone that slipped under me. I was running breathlessly and started to perceive the sound of an aeroplane lingering threateningly overhead.

The sound was repeated, and there came a new and stronger

explosion. It was one of those that feel so close no matter where you are standing, so strong that the ground shook, tiles fell off the roofs and windows out of their frames. It turned out that the first bomb had been dropped over the end of the town, more than two kilometres away. But the second one was really close, falling on the slope opposite the house. And the ground shook again, more violently.

In the meantime I found myself in the cellar – I do not myself know why, since it was safer to stay in the woods outside the town, which was in chaos. My sister and mother pressed against me, screaming, not knowing whether to run or to stay where they were. Tiles kept on falling with a dreadful noise. It seemed as though the house was falling apart as dust welled out from every corner.

Our landlady Hanifa Č., dressed in an outsize red jogging suit, was slapping her thighs, alternately calling forlornly to her husband Vahid, who was too lazy to budge despite the bombs, or shouting: 'Shame on you!' at the planes. Everything was over soon, after five or maybe ten minutes. Still shivering with fear, we emerged from the cellar. Scared and mistrustful we raised our heads, not believing that the planes were gone. If anything was worse than the shock of an explosion and the elemental fear of losing your life, then it was the awareness that so little stood between you and death – mere minutes or seconds.

After leaving the cellar, we went round the neighbourhood calling to those in nearby courtyards, who were doing just the same, to check if everyone was alive. But we did not dare go too far from the cellar entrance. We had just started pulling ourselves together when the first information on casualties arrived. The only casualties from the attack, carried out by two Yugoslav MIGs, had been a woman and a child. Mother and son had both been standing a couple of metres from the explosion when the bomb hit the concrete of the school playground. What remained of them had to be scraped off the ground with shovels.

Three weeks later another attack took place. The planes were more precise and the pilots more bloodthirsty, targeting the centre of the town. The day before the attack, my family had moved into a flat next to the market, in a building that looked as if it had been carved into the hill. Between the entrance to the building and the steep hill there was only a narrow and permanently cold passage. It was right there that my mother and my sister found themselves when the planes appeared above the town.

The fog had just dispersed, the day was clear and from the safety of their machines they had the town in full view. When the first bomb was dropped, I was in the flat and started running down – this time down the stairs – to the shelter. The building shook dangerously. But unlike with the previous explosions, this time there was a sharp smell in the air and both corridor and staircase were soon filled with black smoke. I thought of my mother and sister who were outside at the fountain, but there was no way to find out where they were until the planes left.

People were standing in the stairwell, coughing heavily from the smoke. Others were running down the stairs or going back to their flats to get family members who had stayed behind. I pushed my way through the crowd and entered the dark cellar. One could not see anything in there, but loud and agitated breathing could be heard despite the throng. I bumped into someone and, since I could not see his face, I asked if he knew where my family was. Mother recognised my voice and pushed towards me from a corner. Both she and my sister were crying. The latter looked inconsolable as my mother told me in one breath what had happened.

The two of them had just got into the building, carrying canisters of water, when the bomb fell next to the building. I could not help thinking that if it had been their turn to fill up the canisters just a moment later, if they had left to get water or woken up just a moment later, a mere moment that might have seemed irrelevant, they would both be dead.

In the commotion, mother had lost her headscarf, her greying hair was untidy and her face was flushed and red, both from agitation and from running. My sister was sobbing, clinging onto mother's trousers. Like all the other children she was shivering and looking up at us, asking for protection or at least an explanation. And we could not offer her either.

Despite the fact that the bombs had fallen onto the most densely populated area of town, there were no fatalities. We soon moved again, this time to grandfather in the countryside. We stayed there for two months and the planes dropped their deadly load over Srebrenica at least twice more. They were jet planes. They flew over the town at high speed, breaking the sound barrier with a terrifying bang, and then dropped bombs during their next pass, only to disappear as quickly as they had appeared. It all happened with lightning speed, which made it easier for us to bear those attacks. But it made us feel just as powerless, so that we could not react until everything was over.

We lived through those attacks without ever truly understanding what was going on, as if drunk with fear. The sight of demolished buildings, of human bodies shredded by bombs, of the big craters made by *krmače*, all that horror only got through to us once it had become irrelevant. The worst of it all was the fact that something of that kind could become irrelevant.

But something else left us with enough, or even too much, time to think. The arrival of some planes was announced by the buzz of their engines. Because of that buzz, we disparagingly nicknamed 'mosquitoes' those sporting or farming planes, which the Serbs had equipped with machine-guns and stuffed with bombs. They would circle above the town sometimes for half an hour, looking for a target, flying too high to be shot at. When they turned up for the first time that summer, the pilots insolently flew so low over houses and trenches that their faces were visible.

They flew slowly, carrying a load generally of one or at most two heavy bombs. They flew over not only from Bratunac but also from Serbia, from an airfield on the Tara range, and bombed towns and villages or frontlines in the southern part of the enclave. Bombs and guns were not their deadliest weapons: it was the sound, for it drove into the brain and stayed in the ears. It took days to get rid of that sound, and it reappeared as soon as you lay down and closed your eyes, thinking you were surrounded by complete silence. And you could never know if you were imagining it, or if a 'mosquito' really had appeared somewhere on the horizon and you could not see it.

The 'boilers', as we called their improvised bombs, were very destructive. Fortunately for us they were not that precise, since they were dropped from a great height and generally exploded on one of the slopes near town. But the one that hit a school building, maybe the only one that got close to its target, literally ripped the building in two: its smaller part was still standing, but now separated from the rest of the building by a gap as large as a hand. We could not grasp why they targeted that abandoned building – why most of the bombs fell close to it.

We tried in vain to find some explanation, or we put it down to coincidence, but still my friends and I went less often to the school library from which we were accustomed to take out piles of books. With increasing fear we would creep through corridors and classrooms, getting in through broken windows and stepping over shards of glass. Listening to the sky, we stopped breathing at every rustle and were ever quicker to leave the building. We knew that nothing good for us came out of the sky.

Shivering with cold, they waited every morning in long queues, regardless of their gender and age, of their social status and wealth, of their education and upbringing. Their pasts had by then become insignificant. They stood there, waiting for their turn, stamping cold feet to warm them up. Clouds of steam coming out of their mouths, they chatted with each other, even if they were often complete strangers – though eventually we would all know one another. Sometimes hours passed before they got a couple of steps closer to the entrance of the small yellow building in the centre of the town, on whose roof stood a huge aerial.

Some tried to imagine how, soon after they entered one of the gloomy rooms of that single-storey building, their voice would travel through the air. A second or two later, from somewhere – God knows where – the voices of their daughters, sons, brothers, wives who had left the town or the country would arrive. There was a busy throng in there, with people continually coming in and out. From behind constantly opening doors, scraps of other people's conversations were to be heard: 'Almasa, can you hear me? How are you doing there, can you hear me?'

And then a man would come out from inside, hiding tears or angry at the radio operator who could not give him longer than five minutes. Others would then come in and happily take their place at the front of the queue, which had by then formed in the little room as well. The man who operated the rickety army-green radio set would then check his watch, turn to them and ask, more to make sure than because he really wanted to hear the answer: 'It's Banovići's turn now, is that right?'

He would then turn round and start what in their ham-radio-operator jargon was called 'calling through': 'Here Tango-Alpha-Sierra-Four, Tango-Alpha-Sierra-Four, are you there Whiskey-Bravo-Delta?' He would try to speak louder than the noise made by the people in the room. He would turn the bulky black wheel on the machine, changing 'bands'. (Ah, how familiar we were back then with that terminology! So many of us had gone home sad and disappointed, because some Mike-Golf-Charlie was not on the 'band'!) A wailing sound similar to a whistle would jar on the ears, until from the other end another voice was audible, whether male or female it was impossible to say.

– 'Tango-Alpha-Sierra-Four, I'm here,' was heard through the interference.

– 'Is everyone there?'

– 'Yes they are,' said the voice from the other end, 'shall we start?'

The operator, a young man with messy, or at least never neatly combed, blonde hair, would then ask: 'Is there a Fadila at your end?' Then at last another operator's voice would say: 'Yes, is there a Mirsad there?'

The latter would come closer, sit down in a wobbly chair, and Fadila doubtless did the same. Then, after a short explanation on how to use the station, along the lines of: 'Press this when you're talking and let go when you're listening', he would utter a simple: 'Fadila, how are you doing?' In ideal conditions, when there was no interference or deafening static and the voice did not arrive distorted and altered, he would then reply in the same tone. Questions mostly concerned their whereabouts and how they were doing, how the children were doing, parents, family, close and distant relatives.

No one ever said: 'I love you'. Never did an open love declaration pass through those wires, aerials and cables. And yet nowhere and never had there been more love concentrated on one spot than in that half-dark, grey room with bars on the windows.

People came from the remotest parts of the enclave. They travelled for days, on foot or horseback, hoping to speak to their relatives. Many did not even know where their families were. On arriving in the town disappointment hit them when they realised that they first had to put their name down on an ever longer list – the longest in the world, I'd say – get an appointment and then come back in a week, two weeks, sometimes even a month.

It took a long time before the radio station was accessible to everyone. At the very beginning of the war, at the time of the mass deportations, the most important thing was to find out if their loved ones were alive. People gathered in front of the post-office building while the phones were still working, or round ham-radio operators, to look for the names of their family members and relatives on the long lists of people who had arrived in the territory controlled by the Army of Bosnia-Herzegovina.

If they had survived April 1992, they were generally in Tuzla or its vicinity, in refugee camps in Banovići, Živinice, Srebrenik, Gračanica etc. If they had left the country, it took months before their names appeared on the list, and the hope that they were alive lessened by the day.

In the meantime, in autumn 1992 as winter drew closer, it became possible even to have conversations with them. After a conversation, impoverished people gratefully offered everything they had to the young radio operators who had made it possible. They offered food although they had none themselves. It was often their last would-be mouthful, but the men would refuse it despite the fact that they were themselves skin and bones. The village people were unstinting: 'racks' of dried meat would protrude from their pockets, or they would have brought eggs, cheese or a slaughtered hen as a gift.

The mouths of the refugees would water as they tried not to stare into the abundance of their bags. They would search inside their coats, looking for a bundle of tobacco, possibly paid for with their last savings, in order to show that they too had brought something, no matter how modest. But – they carried on with their interior monologue – had they stayed in their homes, they would have brought a roasted lamb, no, better – an ox. Wives would have made big pots of coffee to be given out in the morning to people chilled to the bones. Ah, if only they had stayed at home … And then someone from the front of the queue was called in and they made a step forward, still standing behind the farmer with the heavy bag.

We were starving, but in winter 1992 it became almost easier to cope with the lack of food than with the total absence of salt. Food, or rather what we called food – and at that time we were eating bread made of ground apple skins among other things – had long become unbearably bland. There was no salt anywhere, not even on the market where one could buy everything, including wheat and dried meat … Both bread and meat were unsalted. Peasants who came to town reported how their cows and horses would go mad after a month without salt. We were becoming more and more like animals, as if the salt was the only thing that had once made the difference between animals and us.

In the middle of winter something suddenly appeared that at the time looked like possible salvation. I do not know how and by whom it was discovered that the raw unrefined salt that was once strewn onto frozen roads could be put to use. I also do not know who found, or where, the first unused stone-like lump of that salt. But almost everyone found some way to get one. They were brought home black and dirty in plastic bags, to then be long boiled before use. Sometime it took hours before the last trace of the dirt that had accumulated on the surface disappeared in the boiling water. Each layer was carefully removed, new water was poured on, then a new layer of dirt removed. We waited patiently until a thin, but snowy white, dried crust of salt appeared at the bottom of a pot, pan, cauldron or whatever. We then frantically sprinkled food with salt, as if wanting to make up for all those past months without – and not knowing that we were poisoning ourselves. Poisoning may be the wrong word: the salt we were using contained no iodine, the lack of which caused goitre. This disease remains a mystery to me, but I do know that it apparently has something to do with the thyroid gland. Several such cases were indeed registered.

Little changed later on, when the UNHCR started supplying the town after it was declared a 'safe zone' in April 1993. In the convoys that arrived from Belgrade (for that is where the UNHCR headquarters for the whole of eastern Bosnia, hence also for Srebrenica, were situated) there was almost no salt. UNHCR workers kept on promising a convoy of salt that would solve all the problems. The Serbs might not have known exactly what was going on in the town and how acute the lack of salt was, but they did prevent every convoy with a substantial quantity of salt from entering the enclave.

Municipal officials in Srebrenica were frustrated. They threatened humanitarian workers, claiming that they were Serb spies, but to no avail. Actually there was just enough salt to keep permanent the fear of running out, and the price of one kilo at a constant 50 Deutschmarks.

The authorities were nervous not just because they were concerned about the population. Everyone knew that the salt sold on the market could come only from humanitarian aid; just as it was obvious that key figures of the municipal hierarchy were getting rich precisely from the illegal sale of humanitarian aid.

All types of military operations in Srebrenica were called 'actions'. Every time the Serbs attacked the enclave it was naturally called an attack. But when forces of the Army of Bosnia-Herzegovina, in forays out of the enclave or expanding the enclave's boundaries, attacked Serb positions or liberated what used to be purely Muslim villages, that was called an action.

It was usually known in advance when some action would take place, which forces would be taking part, and where it would be carried out. And during long get-togethers even the exact starting-point of an action was guessed with great accuracy. A day or two beforehand, there would always be strange goings-on in the town, and more soldiers there than usual. They would leave a day in advance on open-topped trucks, singing *Poljem se širi miris ljiljana* [The scent of lilies fills the meadow] – many leaving never to come back.

During battles, soldiers mostly recognised each other by coloured bands tied round arms or on shoulders, the colours changing with every new operation. After the battle ended, each went his own way. There was no storage depot for seized ammunition or food. On paper there was one, but it was always empty because the soldiers – and the civilians who accompanied them in every action – took the war booty straight home.

As time passed the number of civilians accompanying military actions rose, and by the end of the first war year there would be several times more civilians than soldiers. They would patiently wait for the first bunker to fall or for the first Serb soldiers to start running away. And then they would run after them, sometimes even during the battle, screaming, banging on pots and pans, basically making a blood-chilling racket. From a thousand throats would resound 'Allahu-ekber!', and that scream would not only scare the Serbs but also create the impression of numerical superiority. These civilians perished in even greater numbers than soldiers. Women wanting to grab an extra piece of food ended up running into crossfire; children sought shelter from airplane bombs under trees; unarmed men ran into gun barrels.

I had known Senad Mašić my whole life. He, his younger brother Sead and I grew up together. We spent our summers on the banks of the Drina, getting bruises running after a football, something for which I had no talent whatsoever in comparison with Sead.

Unlike the latter, Senad was introverted, withdrawn, taciturn and a somewhat pale and weak boy. As we grew up, our lives went different ways: they went to school in Bratunac, I went to school in Srebrenica; they were both average students, I enjoyed my swot reputation; they both still played football, I started playing basketball.

But none of those differences could have lessened the shock I felt when I heard that Senad had been killed. What made it even worse was the fact that a day earlier, just one day earlier, I had talked to him on the street. I did not know, or he did not want to tell me, that the next day he was going to Loznička Rijeka, a place marked for the next attack by the enclave forces. Maybe he did not know himself.

Two days later, which was how long it took for the news to arrive, I heard that he had perished as he tried to run away from airplane bombs. He was carrying a sack of flour on his back, a bag of white, finely ground, silky flour as big as his whole life.

Those who saw soldiers off to the battle, their wives, sisters and girlfriends, threw water behind them, probably out of superstition. Anxiously they said prayer after prayer, waiting for the news that always seemed to arrive before the outcome of the battle was really decided.

The success of a particular action was announced by the firing that would come closer to the town: soldiers who survived celebrated by shooting in the air. Those who had not participated in the battle came out on the streets to greet them, shaking their heads at the waste of ammunition.

Military setbacks were rare in the summer of 1992, but they too were just as reliably announced by the unnatural silence that shrouded the town. Amid silent weeping, the dead were buried in numerous new cemeteries. But worse than the dead were the wounded. They lay in hospitals without medication, without hope of recovery, and the doctors could only pray for them. The hospital was the only building I did not go into during that horrible war. My stomach could not bear the foul odour, the smell of rotten human flesh that permeated the hospital. Doctors could not even give the simplest infusion.

On the occasion of one of the numerous attacks on *Zvijezda* [Star] – the high ground between Potočari and Bratunac, named after the massive red star with Tito's signature cut out of sheet metal that used to adorn it before the war – a desperate brother of one of the wounded tearfully offered a cow for an infusion pack. One pack. No one seemed interested in a deal like that.

There is no reliable record of the number of actions, because many were probably planned in too much haste and carried out without having been previously put down on paper. I think that was done only for those major, grandiose actions (by the going standards) involving a thousand or at the most two thousand soldiers.

Because of the high number of casualties, such large actions were avoided by those commanding a multitude of units whose sole common denominator was the fact that they at least formally belonged to the Army of Bosnia-Herzegovina. At least during the first days of the war, the command focused on small, isolated outposts which could be liberated without too much effort, and which would bring precious ammunition, weapons and food. Big operations followed only at the beginning of winter, when the population had to be fed. And where there were plenty of Serb soldiers, food was unfailingly to be found. The liberated territory was spreading and it was getting more and more difficult to keep control over it.

The Serbs also understood that a bunch of badly armed and poorly dressed guerrilla fighters was threatening to become an army. In the spring of 1993 they decided to deal far more seriously with Srebrenica, which by then meant a territory stretching from Rogatica nearly all the way up to Zvornik.

A yellow truck with an open trailer stopped in the centre of the market, which was always the busiest place in town. Four soldiers quickly opened the trailer and jumped out, two more stepping out of the cabin. One of them who was clearly in charge, with blonde, almost white hair, took out a pistol from a holster and stopped for a moment, looking around. Shouting savagely and pointing his gun, he started ordering the men who happened to be there to get onto the truck.

He did not tolerate disobedience, hitting anyone who resisted. His companions were equally brutal, faithfully following his every move. Older men came out of the shade of nearby buildings and climbed onto the trailer, shaking their heads in disbelief. In about ten minutes, the trailer was filled with scared people. The truck started off and disappeared in the same direction it had come from. Later that afternoon we all knew and no one needed to tell us that they had ended up on the frontline.

This happened nearly every week during the summer: the same yellow truck would stop on the busiest street in town, soldiers would jump out, arrest everyone who happened to be there, then drive them to the front. Usually to the hottest frontline of the moment, in Likari, a village north of the town on a hill that was crucial in controlling the road between Srebrenica and Potočari in the northern part of the enclave.

What the Western press called the Bosnian Army – and what the Serbs feared so much – was actually at that time in Srebrenica a few disconnected groups. Their common denominator was their hostility to the Serbs. From time to time they jointly attacked important Serb targets or helped each other in resisting Serb attacks.

Because of this method of organisation, or rather because of the lack of it, most of the battle-fit population was not enrolled in the army. There were no conscription lists. On the other hand, there were not enough weapons for those who enrolled in the army voluntarily. During the whole of 1992 military police, or rather a group of thugs who called themselves military police, supplemented units on the front. They kidnapped people from the street in broad daylight, pointing pistols at them and then taking them to the front regardless of their age and in the clothes they happened to be wearing.

It did not matter that no one knew who the military police represented and why they were allowed to break the law. Without any scruple they sent people to their deaths, not telling them where they were being sent, while these people had no idea where they were being taken and were completely lost once they finally got there.

When they eventually got to the front, other soldiers shoved weapons into the hands of those scared people and said: 'The Serbs are over there!', pointing to the Serb trenches. They were generally kept there for seven days until a truck came from town, full of equally lost and scared people picked up from the streets.

There were men of all ages. Some were in their twenties, some were under-age boys, and some were men in their fifties who instead of claiming exemption on the grounds of age silently accepted their fate.

Few trucks drove through the town in those months, and it was always obvious which one was dangerous because it would somehow move more ominously than the rest. Out of nowhere, it would appear behind the town café and drive slowly past the department store, circling around on the lookout for victims. Men ran into hallways, fled into flats. The policeman who was always in charge of the action, a young, thin-lipped man with completely white hair and deathly pale skin, ran after them into buildings, setting his men an example. They followed him, smashed down doors, searched flats and threw furniture over, pulling out people hidden in wardrobes, under sofas or beds, or locked in toilets.

From the street this little war moved into houses and flats, into buildings that the policemen searched thoroughly from the cellar upwards, not forgetting the roof. Hunted men, who generally cursed having been born as men, soon found a new way of avoiding this sort of people-hunting.

Instead of waiting in their houses and hoping that the round-up would pass them by that day, they fled onto slopes covered in small bushes above the town. From up there, they observed the panic on the streets, which must have looked silly from that viewpoint. And soldiers kept searching for people in houses; they caught them on the street and in front of their families; they forced them to get onto the truck, humiliated. Sometimes they got so carried away with their task that they paid no attention to whom they were forcing onto the truck.

At one point it became clear to everyone how counter-productive kidnapping people off the street was: instead of fighting Serb soldiers, civilians now hid from Bosnian ones, shunning both the front and the army that sent them to their death in such an unscrupulous manner. No one wanted to be chased into a battle where the odds were high that you would not come back. We all wanted at least an illusion of choice, a chance to keep our honour safe, if not to stay alive.

I saw what it was like with my own eyes. My uncle, who was picked up off the street, ran back from the front scared and covered in blood, fleeing on the occasion of one of the strongest Serb attacks on that part of the front. The next time the truck turned up in our neighbourhood, my father just silently picked up his things and got onto the trailer himself, so thatI should not end up on the front.

It was only in late 1992 or early 1993 that at least some of the men were 'drafted', as it used to be called in the jargon of the former Yugoslav army. I watched some of them walk to the front in groups of about ten, carrying empty rucksacks on their backs, wearing patched clothes and ducking when a shell flew over them.

You got back home, tired as you always were when you got back from the front. You had walked ten kilometres after you had been given a breakfast in the morning of a tiny piece of yellow cooked pumpkin, no bigger than the palm of your hand. You had spent the whole night in the trench, listening hard and clutching onto a hunting rifle. You had two bullets in the barrel and two more in your pocket. If the Serbs had attacked that night, you would not have survived. You were not supposed to survive anyway. Your role consisted of giving the alarm by firing two shots and then maybe two more, before they killed you, alone on the hill with the nearest bunker fifty metres away. But they did not attack and you survived the night.

You got home, tired as you always were. She would be making lunch. You were always on time for the meal, they say this characteristic followed you all your life. Wherever you went, on a sudden visit to people you had not seen for a while or briefly popping over to your neighbours, they would always be just laying the table. Taking care not to miss a single crumb, you would greedily eat corn bread possibly made out of the same corn you used to pour so lavishly into your cow's trough before the war. You would sip hot water of an indeterminate whitish colour, and greedily search for another piece of potato at the bottom of the dish, in vain. Then you would go to the sofa, she would be sitting in the middle. You would kneel down, maybe it reminded you of your youth, and put your head in her lap. You were just over forty, but your hair had already gone grey and the round bald spot on the top of your head was making unstoppable progress.

The children were already grown up, they would be somewhere outside when you arrived. Anyway, you liked to think that you two had the right to some time on your own. You did not want them to watch her take out a comb and start running it carefully through your hair. She would slowly run it through, then put it down on the table, searching on its fine teeth for small, shiny lice that would still be twitching their countless legs. They would be swollen with your blood and crack loudly as she squeezed them against the edge of the table, using her hardened nail. They only left a small, barely visible, bloody stain on the white surface.

Each time this would take a while, and each time you would bring a multitude of lice back from the front, from stuffy dormitories. When she was done with the lice, she would put down the comb and search with her hands for nits, killing them in your hair by squeezing them between two nails. Tired, you would get up, your rheumatic knees unable to bear further kneeling and your stiff back aching. You would heat up the water in the pot on the stove, thinking of your boy. He had walked a couple of kilometres into the woods that day, chopped down a tree and dragged it back, then pushed it down the slope rising above the house. He had dragged it up the steep stairs to the garden entrance, chopped it up, cut it into small pieces and stacked the split logs against the house wall.

You bathed in the dark bathroom. Of all the places in the world, you thought, it gets dark first in Srebrenica; of all the houses in the town, it gets dark first in this one; of all the rooms in the house – in the bathroom. You turned on the light, or rather lit the tip of a cloth protruding from a petrol-filled pot and took it to the mirror. You looked at your pock-marked face, at the large folds of skin hanging from where fat once used to be. You opened your mouth and saw the gaps between your teeth. You put a hand into your mouth, searched for a loose, yellowed tooth in your upper set of teeth and pulled it out. No blood came out of the hole that the tooth left behind. You knew you were going to die.

*M*eals Ready to Eat. We also called them *Meals Rejected by Ethiopians*, in a dark and ironic attempt to make fun of our own situation. After the Serbs once again defeated the world in the spring of 1993 – for the nth time in the three years of the enclave – and after the world failed to gather enough courage to help us survive, the American administration started supplying the enclave from the air. Since the first operation started at a time when the Serbs were still advancing towards the town in spring 1993, the first palettes of food landed on their positions, which had changed in the course of the night. We were embittered towards the people who for years had refused to help us, even though we were on the verge of disappearing; and who, when they finally decided to make a move that carried no risk, were not even able to do it properly.

At ground level, things had hardly ever been worse. Thousands of people wandered outside the town at night, carrying torches, everyone driven by their own instinct or urged on by someone else, since we never knew exactly where and when the food would be dropped. We called what was dropped simply and unimaginatively: 'packages'. Listening intently, freezing next to a puny fire, we would remain empty-handed nearly as often as we actually got anything. The planes sometimes went to Žepa, sometimes to Goražde, sometimes they simply did not come. We would then leave, disappointed and with our heads bowed.

On those nights when the planes did shed their rain, we would scatter throughout the hills above the town, running for food, firmly gripping empty bags and rucksacks, or clutching their straps as they swung empty on our backs.

The sound would slowly come closer, so loud that the first whistles of the massive palettes falling was not heard at all. Everyone would take shelter under trees, but then, after a series of dull, penetrating sounds which signalled that the palettes had started to land, total chaos would break out. Everyone ran to the spot where they thought the palettes were, not paying attention to whether they had all landed, sometimes actually attracted by new sounds. Several people even perished in this way, smashed by the several-hundred-kilo weight of the heavy palettes – which landed, moreover, in the most inaccessible spots, as if someone had planned it like that.

You had to stay alive while wandering on the slopes at night, then find the way to get out of the woods. More than once I slid down the snowy slopes on my bottom, not knowing where exactly I was going and what was waiting for me down there. If I got lost in the dark that was the only way to get back, since I was certain that going down the hill would take me back to town.

In a way, it was our war within a war. During the day we fought against the Serbs, and during the night we fought against each other for every bit of food, for one plastic packet. For the nth time people lost all their scruples, went beyond all limits of human behaviour, once again losing all dignity. The fight for survival had acquired yet another form.

A friend of mine, who somehow always came off better than me in those nocturnal hunts, told me one night how he nearly got killed as he was trying to get hold of an entire palette of food. He and two friends happened to be near the spot where a couple of palettes had landed. In the darkness they saw a boy standing next to one still unopened palette.

– 'Kid, what are you doing there?' one of them asked, just to make sure what was going on.

– 'I'm keeping guard on the palette,' the kid replied, his voice ringing with a note of responsibility.

– 'Come on, get lost!' one of them shouted, trying to scare off the kid.

– 'Daddy, these three are bothering me!' the kid screamed.

Then the reloading of a weapon was heard from the darkness a couple of steps behind the palette. Defeated, the three left the boy with his booty, knowing that had they moved a step closer to the palette, the father would not have hesitated for a second to open fire on them.

Planes also dropped individual packages. We guessed that the idea was to provide as many people as possible with food, which was quite right. But it was a tiring task: as the packets of food wrapped in plastic rained down, people greedily dug in the snow, collecting them and not lifting their heads for hours. Sometimes, after a generous delivery, I found myself among the hundreds of people who days later still walked through the woods and dug in the snow with long sticks, looking for deeply buried packages or ones too well hidden to be found straight away.

When today I say 'packages', I always think first of those that were dropped during the initial weeks, containing food from American military reserves. There is another good reason for that: they were always the easiest ones to carry. They were packages of twelve meals, light and tightly packed. The loads soon became more varied. Planes started dropping food from British military reserves (at one point, someone found a British box of biscuits from 1968), then cardboard packs with instruction manuals in German and later in Italian.

That was the best way for us to tell them apart, and to measure who among us had a better or bigger haul. In that respect American packages were the least appreciated, because they were not very varied. The German and Italian ones were always considered some little reward for the 'invested effort', because they were the most generous; the British ones did not even enter the competition.

The tears that well up when I think of those times are sometimes interrupted by a smile. In the darkness some rare comic situation will gleam, or rather some interruption to the cruel fight for survival, the eternal Bosnian perplexity and measureless capacity for endurance – and simply make all three easier to bear.

In early 1993 during yet another invasion of the town by refugees, a family of four arrived in my neighbourhood from the vicinity of Cerska. They had been exiled to Cerska previously from somewhere close to Nova Kasaba, a little town on the road from Sarajevo to Srebrenica. That they had been in exile for a while was best illustrated by the fact that they were all – husband, wife and two daughters – terribly thin.

When humanitarian help started being delivered from the air, the father carried back as much as he could every night, like everyone else. On one occasion, in the course of just one night, he went back to the woods several times and brought several big 50 kg sacks of white powder, which he like everyone else took for flour. His wife made bread out of that powder for the next couple of weeks. Very rapidly all the members of the family put on weight and the girls' cheeks became red again. I do not know how, I do not even know what the medical explanation is, but it turned out to be thanks to the white powder that their mother used for bread. As a matter of fact, it was not flour – but milk powder.

The first convoy of humanitarian help arrived in Srebrenica in December 1992, escorted by UN forces. With the convoy a couple of journalists arrived as well, who were given a deadline by the Serbs: they had to leave the town before noon, otherwise it would be shelled. When the long column of trucks stopped on Učina Bašča in front of the big bakery, a crowd of curious people gathered on both sides of the street. The crowd looked only half as exotic and unbelievable to the journalists and soldiers as they did to it.

The former were wearing rags, the latter their warm winter clothes; the former were pale, starved and frozen, the latter ruddy and bursting with health as they tentatively stepped out of their heavily armoured cars. For the population, these strangers were the last hope, really the last, because this convoy had arrived just as the reserves of food were almost completely gone. The people were surprised, even offended, that these newcomers did not show the same amount of interest as they did in them. On the contrary, all the journalists flocked around Naser Orić – unmissable on such occasions – trying to get a good quote. 'Neutrality' was the word of the day, but the two British tabloid journalists talking to Orić were certainly not able to differentiate between objectivity and neutrality.

The convoy mostly contained flour and big tins of paté, which were distributed a couple of days later: one part to civilians and the other to soldiers preparing for the next action. Bread made out of wheat flour was such an enormous novelty that it was painful to the eyes at first glimpse, and also to the unaccustomed stomach; but that did not last long – three or four days only.

For the next couple of months, up to March 1993, Srebrenica was lonely again, left to its own devices. Bloody battles were still being fought for the town, and it was only at the beginning of March that convoys were let through the barricades again. Trucks stayed in town for one night and sacks of flour were unloaded. They were then replaced by women and children who were lucky enough (at least, that was thought at the time) to leave the town the next day. It was only after the 'safe zone' had been declared that the supply of humanitarian help became steady.

Convoys came once, twice, sometimes three times a week and brought all sorts of things: from flour and less often salt to juice powder and 'Ikar' brand cans, clothes, footwear, cleaning products, soap – and sometimes quite useless items.

When the Serbs wanted to make the local population nervous, or wanted to put pressure either on Srebrenica or on the government in Sarajevo, they did not let convoys through their barricades for days on end. On one such occasion, after a month had passed without a single convoy arriving and the reserves of food were running seriously low, a convoy of six Russian trucks unexpectedly and noisily entered the town.

Completely desperate, I watched from the post-office window how the atmosphere in town instantly got much livelier, just like every time a convoy arrived. I realised how dependent we were on those increasingly occasional, indeed haphazard, deliveries. But this time the bigger than usual crowd, observing the unloading in front of the department-store warehouse, was bitterly disappointed when the contents were discovered to be tons of ironware and soap.

A large proportion of humanitarian aid ended up on the town market the very next day: stalls would be full of shiny packets of orange-juice powder or big tins of oil. The authorities were kindly disposed to it. Actually, only once did the police carry out a raid and arrest the people trading in humanitarian aid.

The chief of police Hakija Meholjić threatened: 'I'm remembering it all, and the time will come when I'll speak out!' But the traders were soon released from prison and everything went on just as before. In the summer of 1994, a protest broke out in front of the town hall: people accused the president of the municipality and his staff of stealing humanitarian help, which affected the ordinary people. On that same night, the leader of the protest was killed. The town was silenced. The practice went on: part of the aid was distributed to the population, and the other – better quality – part ended up on the market or in private warehouses belonging to town officials. They chose the quantity and type of goods they were interested in from the central warehouse. There were all sorts of things for officers, town officials, their wives and mistresses, including new trainers or the odd pair of Levi's that had somehow strayed into the humanitarian aid.

Under the guise of humanitarian work, all kinds of dilettantes also arrived in town. Some of them pretended to be spies and introduced themselves as such; others were humanitarian workers; and some wanted to help but did not know how.

In autumn 1994, an official of the International Red Cross, a Swiss, who introduced himself to Orić as an employee of the American governmental agency Omega Thor, taught close combat to Orić's soldiers in a burnt-out village near Srebrenica. I nearly burst out laughing as he pulled a business card out of his pocket.

In the spring of 1995, at a regular meeting of international organisations that was held every morning, two recently arrived female workers from Norwegian People's Aid presented the following idea: contraception and the sex education of the population. They were willing to ask their organisation to send a supply of several thousand condoms. By then, rumours that people were starving had started spreading again.

Several elderly people allegedly even starved to death in a prefabricated settlement in Slapovići, but it was never fully investigated. If it did indeed happen, the town authorities were the ones to blame. For after the fall of the town it was discovered that some of the warehouses in the town were full of food. In July 1995, after a couple of days of Serb attacks, as the situation was already descending into chaos, the population broke into warehouses to find them full. I remember a bent old man struggling to carry a sack of flour, I suppose, while another man went into the warehouse to get another sack out.

The army, or what was supposed to be the army, had already started leaving the town, and I still cannot recreate that feeling of forlornness that overcame me as I watched those people carrying out food from the cold warehouses, as if they were stealing it, stealing it from the death that would soon catch up with them.

In March 1993, thousands of people left the town with UNHCR convoys. Crammed on truck trailers, piled on top of each other, wearing all the clothes they possessed and with a couple of bags in which they were supposed to fit their whole lives, they set off on a journey of several hundred kilometres. Exposed to the insults of Serb soldiers and civilians during the journey, they left the town whose end was palpable, on open and dirty trucks, leaving behind their loved ones.

Only women and children under eighteen could get on those trucks, but occasionally someone dared to defy destiny and send older children out of town. The Serbs checked the trucks carefully, often forcing everyone to get out and letting them climb back onto those high trailers once the inspection was done. As they passed by civilians threw stones at them, while inside the trucks a battle for survival was fought: people were literally sitting and lying down on top of each other. Several children had suffocated by the end of the journey.

People were panicking and everyone wanted to get their place in the trailer as soon as possible. The authorities tried to organise the evacuation so that it would run as smoothly as possible: they 'assigned' a certain number of trucks to each village, each area of the town, and only women and children from there could get onto those trucks.

There was an indescribable commotion and no one could be certain that they would manage to 'cram' their family onto a truck, thus in a way getting a weight off their minds, a weight too heavy for those times. This meant staying alone and being happy that you had done so, knowing that you had got a family member to safety.

In the midst of the general chaos the first victims of evacuation fell: a local commander killed a woman who had mistakenly got onto a truck that he considered 'his' by throwing her from the trailer onto frozen concrete. By the very next day footprints had appeared upon the dried bloodstains. Life had priority over death and people had no time for compassion.

One of the local interpreters was arrested on the charge of receiving a bribe for 'arranging a loading' onto a truck. He denied it, but a policeman searched him and found 200 DM in his pocket. He claimed that a woman had just tucked the money into his pocket, but it was too late. He got special treatment during custody: the police held him in an isolation cell and beat him relentlessly. Partly because they envied him, partly because they were revolted by his act.

Despite everything, the evacuation continued but with less and less order. Drowsy Swedish truck drivers, who had driven humanitarian aid into town the day before and spent the night on the parking lot in front of the secondary-school building, would be even more confused and scared by the armed guard they would wake up to see standing by their trucks. The soldiers would first take care of their own families, then of the families of their relatives, friends and acquaintances. Some would be lifting women and children off the ground, while others would be hoisting them up and placing them in the trailer until they themselves could no longer stand up straight in the crush.

After my father died in December 1992, I insisted that my mother and sister at least try to get a place on a truck. My only plan was to stay in town, because I was certain that it would be easier to take care of myself alone, knowing they were both safe. They stubbornly refused, especially mother, whose crying fits ended our frequent arguments on whether they should leave. I wept too, because it was suddenly my responsibility to take care of them – and they were the only thing I had in my life – in a situation where our lives were worthless and all three of us were totally vulnerable.

In the end I did manage to persuade them to set off into town together, in the early morning of 31 March. If we managed to get them a place on the truck they would leave the town. If we did not, then we would go back and share the fate of the other tens of thousands of inhabitants of Srebrenica.

Everything happened too fast that morning, we had no time to think about the decision we were taking, which was good in a sense, since I do not think we would have been able to take the decision otherwise.

When we arrived at the square in front of the department store, I asked around and found out that the trucks for us refugees from Bratunac were parked in front of the primary school, a couple of hundred metres further on. We went there and, with what seemed to me incredible good luck, managed to work our way to one of the trucks through the thousands of people gathered around.

On the truck stood Mevludin H., a young man whom I did not know all that well but who used to be in the same unit as my father.

I approached the truck and, although formerly it would have taken me hours to do anything like that, asked without hesitation: 'Mevludin, can my family get on?'

'Yes, no problem, bring them here', he replied.

Mother and sister were right behind me. I first lifted mother onto the truck and then my sister. They were waving from the truck. I took a long look at them before I left, then after a couple of seconds turned back for another look, because I believed this might be the last timeI should see them. But the tarpaulin was on, so I left for home.

The streets are slippery, frozen, and walking is difficult. Tears are gushing from my eyes and bothering me. I do not dare to raise my hand and wipe them away, I am on my own for the first time in my life, this is the first day of my adult life, I am scared someone may see me. The tears filling my eyes start to hamper my view and after a couple of steps I fall over onto hard ice. I reach home, a home that is not mine anyway. I do not greet anyone, the house is empty, there is no one to greet anyway. I throw myself onto the sofa I use for sleeping, a sofa of an indeterminate colour bought with money earned 'during temporary work abroad', money earned in the late seventies on some building site in Libya or Germany. Well, that is the kind of sofa onto which I throw myself full length and start crying, choking with tears.

Two weeks later, I had already started working as an interpreter. I found myself on the other side of quite a different kind of evacuation. For the UN was evacuating those who were severely wounded, and during the last day of the medical evacuation I worked as an interpreter for the team of two doctors who were in charge of the selection.

At the entrance of the hospital, two people in white overcoats were sitting at a school desk. They were both doctors, a manI should soon forget and a woman with short, blonde hair whomI should remember for a long time. They got me a chair and I joined them at the desk. In front of it stood several hundred severely or less severely injured people. They had been standing there since the early morning hours, waiting for the medical inspection.

They approached one by one, unwrapped their bandages and displayed rotten wounds caused by a bullet or a shell. They uncovered their broken bones, leaned on crutches, and stood shivering on one leg as they showed the other leg ripped by shrapnel. They gazed into the female doctor's eyes; followed her hands as they reached out for a pad of white paper, wrote down a diagnosis and then gave it to me. I handed the piece of paper to those who were considered injured enough, then leaned over the desk to say: 'Today at two in the football stadium'. That was where the helicopters carrying the injured to Tuzla took off from.

Many of those who were refused wept. Some of them approached me, offered money and referred to acquaintances, asking for the life-saving white piece of paper that would get them out of Srebrenica. I told all of them that I could not help; that I was just an interpreter, and that if I were askedI should put them all on a helicopter and send them out. It was close to noon and the inspection was drawing to an end. The remaining injured, those who had failed the inspection, refused to leave the flat ground in front of the hospital, hoping that someone would take pity on them after all.

The female doctor had a couple of papers left. She took one, wrote down something illegible and held it out to me, saying: 'You can leave too, if you wish.' I got up and walked through the crowd, the paper burning my sweaty palm. And then I made a decision. I went to a man in the crowd whom I knew as a distant relative of my mother's and said: 'Here you go, Rifet.'

He could not believe it; he limped behind me wanting to thank me. His parents appeared and were also trying to thank me. I felt sick. I felt unbearably sick and I just wanted to find a corner to vomit, to throw up my guts, to throw up all I had seen and been through that day and the days before.

Demilitarisation is a word that entered our lives in spring 1993. A minority of the population considered that it was a nice word for surrender, whilst the majority believed it meant an end to the war. We had no idea what demilitarisation should look like, except that it implied that all soldiers 'surrender their weapons or leave the enclave'.

Of course, nobody had the slightest idea of how to implement this. But soon after a Canadian troop under the UN flag arrived in town, this ceased being a problem. We ended up trusting the UN. Tired of fighting for survival, we abandoned ourselves to other people, becoming totally passive, incapable of taking care of ourselves again, accepting that decisions on our lives were taken outside Srebrenica.

A day after their arrival, the Canadian soldiers set up several posts, fencing them off with barbed wire as a precaution, and started collecting weapons. No one wanted to give up their gun and a ridiculously small amount of weapons were handed over to the Canadians, some old weapons that were out of use and a relatively large number of hand-made guns. The Canadian soldiers smiled sourly as if to say: 'OK, we know you barely managed to defend yourselves, but don't expect us to believe you did it with THIS.'

We are talking here about contraptions made, for instance, out of a piece of water-pipe and a usually larger trigger mechanism, whose user never knew for sure if he would himself survive the firing. At the post in the southern part of town where I lived, besides that kind of weapon, a couple of hand-made bombs and some dynamite were also collected.

Like everyone else, partly out of curiosity and partly because I simply had nothing better to do, I stood amongst the people gathered around the Canadian post that morning. When I got bored, I set off to what used to be an embroidery factory before the war, where most of the Canadian forces were now accommodated. The remaining weaponry handed over by the troops from Srebrenica was stored in the factory courtyard.

From the street and through the barbed wire I could see both tanks, and a 105 mm-calibre howitzer for which there was no ammunition, and an APC fitted with two recoilless guns for which there was neither fuel nor ammunition available. Then there was also what was known as a 'small VBR': a helicopter rocket-launcher mounted on wheels and used as artillery, along with a couple of broken *Ose*. I could not help thinking of the people who had died seizing that weaponry, someone's sons and husbands, people who had never wanted to go to war, but it was precisely war that had cost them their lives.

The 'small VBR' had been seized at Sase, another mine in the vicinity of Srebrenica, as had been the APC. The tanks had been seized at Podravanje, a village in the west of the enclave. Although those weapons clearly could not have any effect on the outcome of the war, we were all terribly happy when they roared through the town. Their value resided in the fact that they were shown around, so that the exhausted population could see them and once again believe that the fight against the Serbs was really possible.

I proceeded to the factory entrance. On my way from home I had decided to try at least to use my modest knowledge of English and talk to one of the soldiers at the entrance.

On my way there I practised my English, and after at least half an hour spent standing across the road, I finally ventured to the other side and went over to a little sentry-box at the entrance to the factory. The guard was from Ontario and, since I was quite good at geography and did not dare ask for a job, we discussed lakes in Ontario. We had a chat and he was somewhat surprised that anyone in Srebrenica should know the names of a number of Canadian lakes, whereas I was surprised that he found that surprising.

– *'Are you from around here?'*
– *'No, I'm a refugee.'*
– *'Where did you learn English?'*
– *'In secondary school. I saw a lot of movies in English, too.'*

I do not know what we were talking about when we were joined at the gate by a small, stocky officer with two stripes on his shoulders indicating his rank of captain.

– *'Captain, are we looking for interpreters? I think we have a guy here who speaks pretty good English.'*

The captain's name was John Little. He said that they (the Canadian battalion, that is) did not need interpreters, but he took me to the PTT where they were looking for one. I spent the first day unoccupied, wandering around the murky rooms of the post office. The following day they needed me in the early morning to translate at a meeting between Naser Orić and the Canadian commanding officer.

I was completely lost and the room started spinning round me when I realised I could not understand a word of the English that the Canadian was speaking. DMZ, APC and a ton of other American military abbreviations that I was hearing for the first time in my life made me lose my grip to such an extent that the interpreter brought by the Canadians from Visoko had to take over the translation. I left the office blushing bright red and completely humiliated. It took me hours to recover.

I was expecting to be fired, but found out a couple of weeks later that I had never been hired in the first place, even though I was working every day. At that point I was lucky, because if I had lost my job then a couple of years laterI should have had a pretty big chance of losing my life too – when demilitarisation would no longer mean anything to anyone anymore.

But even after the process of weapons collection was over, such as it was, the international troops continued to treat the military forces within the enclave as if they still existed. They held meetings with the officers of what used to be the 8th Operational Group and then the 28th Division of the Army of Bosnia-Herzegovina. They asked for help when they needed it, pleaded for concessions, assuming that there were still more than enough weapons left in the enclave.

It turned out that regardless of how many weapons were left in the hands of the people of Srebrenica, it was neither necessary nor sufficient to save the town.

With much less intensity the war continued, despite the UN's belief that a truce was in force. Serb forces regularly raided the enclave and kidnapped people from fields. Snipers shot peasants as they worked their land, killing at least several dozen people in this way over the course of the following two years.

On the other hand, the inhabitants of some villages on the border of the enclave built their own observation posts, just a few hundred metres from the UN ones. Seemingly idle young men from the village would spend entire days there, lying around without doing much, observing Serb positions. Patrols of UN soldiers would pass by, stop and search them for weapons, but always in vain. At night the UN would retreat into their observation posts and the young Bosnian men would become more alert as the Serbs left their trenches.

BOOK TWO

WAR

No community should consider itself above the laws determining human relations. No circumstances justify it. Or do some circumstances maybe, when the biological survival of the community is at stake? I do not have an answer to this question, but I do know that what is generally considered as war in Srebrenica was very dirty, dirtier than anywhere else in Bosnia-Herzegovina. The Serbs treated us like animals and after a while we started behaving like animals.

It was not about two communities each of which believed destroying the enemy was necessary for its own survival. No – it was a war in which one community was sentenced to death in advance.

Right at the beginning of the war, the Serbs transformed the towns and villages under their control around Srebrenica into strongholds. From them the Serbs would emerge to burn Bosniak villages until, by mid May, there was not a single one left round Bratunac and hardly any round Srebrenica. Those rare examples left intact were ones too big for the Serb forces, which still functioned on a territorial basis, or ones where they had encountered resistance offered by some small group. That is how the war started.

The Serbs had chased us down into a town that they had emptied of all food reserves, meagre as they were. We did not have a choice other than to die.

To this day I do not really understand why the Serbs did not invade the town earlier and kill us all. I think it was partly because they themselves started to believe their own propaganda about tens of thousands of Green Berets – a paramilitary formation established before the war by the SDA – in Srebrenica. An equally important reason was the ferocity of the response to their violence, which must have surprised them.

Whatever the reason, after what happened in July 1995 I know what would have become of us in 1992 had it not been for a handful of brave people in Srebrenica.

But a crime is a crime, and it is obvious that some of the people who were defending my life committed acts forbidden by legal and customary norms. I do not want to convict them in advance, they are innocent until proven guilty. I do not want to exempt them from guilt either, because I cannot nor is it my job to do so. I just want to ask one question.

Is a crime really a crime?

Until the war it had been an insignificant, nameless place between Srebrenica and Sase, which provided the workforce for the nearby mine. But as it happens, during the war that insignificant and nameless village became one of those places that was a symbol in the eyes of all, and as a result a disproportionately large amount of blood had to be spilled for it.

It was situated fairly close to town, close enough for the Serbs to mortar the town from there at the beginning of the war, killing people while they were crossing the street or queuing for water on Knjaževac Square, the only source in town.

First a weak report would be heard from the sky – we learnt, maybe incorrectly, that this indicated what was called a 'supplementary charge' [*dopunsko punjenje*]. The long whistle of the shell would be heard, and as it came closer to the ground you could tell by its sound that the shell was rotating around its axis, rending the air. Where these shells hit concrete, they left barely visible holes, along with a sheaf of shrapnel scars spreading in deadly concentric circles. Puddles of blood would spread on the heated asphalt, gather dust, and stay there drying until washed off by the first rain.

Lifeless bodies would lie around, the bodies of children, most often sent for water by their mothers, or of women who hastily and just for a moment had left their kitchens, still with pieces of dough on their hands and their trousers tied with a waist-string. There at the town fountain my schoolfellow Adam Rizvanović too was killed, a boy I remember for his gaze, the most melancholic in the world. He was patiently waiting with the others to pour water

83

into the transparent white canister, of which there were inexcusably many in those months.

The Serb soldiers from Zalazje would regularly remind us of their presence and the price of that presence was increasing. They were constantly there, above the town; we could not even use the paths in the vicinity, which they kept covered. They were too well armed, their trenches were too deep, and the clearings round the village were studded with mines.

In those months armed groups would attack Serb targets. Sometimes these were convoys of trucks carrying Serb soldiers, at other times the groups would launch pirate raids on villages near the front. After every action, without exception, a rain of shells would pour down onto the town from Zalazje. Whether five Serb soldiers got killed in an ambush or two lonely houses were burnt down on some hilltop, the town was unfailingly punished.

As soon as even the tiniest skirmish had begun, retaliation came mercilessly from Zalazje, the shells falling with unusual precision, and lasted long after the clash was over. We suspected that the harder and more intense the shelling became, the heavier their losses must have been and the closer the young men from Srebrenica were to realising their goals.

But 'quiet' days were worse and always brought more victims. One or at most two shells would fall in the course of a day, typically hitting the busiest spot, where people were milling around in the exhausting heat. Their reflexes were numbed by a day-long silence and they perished. Perished as they accidentally stood at the entrance of a building, as they lingered for a moment to greet an acquaintance across the road, as they talked too loudly to hear the noise that was coming closer, believing that everything that day was looking as if no war was on.

On the morning of 30 July 1992, forces from Srebrenica attacked Zalazje. Nearly everyone who could carry a rifle – and who also owned one – set off to the village. By the end of the day, the ashes of the burned houses were cold. The village was attacked from all sides and the roads cut off. One could get out of Zalazje, but not get into it. The help that was sent did not get further than the ambush set up on the road several kilometres from the village.

As I found out later, during that action Naser Orić was lightly wounded by a hand grenade that a Serb soldier threw at him as he tried to enter one of the houses in the village, from which fire was coming. Orić and several of his soldiers had already searched the ground floor and were getting ready to run up to the first floor, when a hand grenade rolled down the stairs, landing right between his legs.

A less highly trained, skilful or cool-headed person would not have survived, becoming a victim of his own fear. But he immediately threw himself backwards towards the entrance of the house, and as he was still rolling the grenade exploded, scattering hundreds of tiny metal balls. A bigger grenade would have killed not only him but also his friends, who got away with somewhat more serious wounds.

The name of that small village is forever engraved into our memory also because of an event that occurred several months later, on the darkest day of the three years of the enclave, a day so dark that it seemed dawn had not broken at all. About forty soldiers were massacred, together with their commander Akif Ustić, at the entrance of the abandoned village, where the forest path reaches a clearing on which houses are scattered.

All that was found was a truck full of bullet-holes and congealed blood, tufts of hair sticky with blood and fragments of bone. The Serbs had shot at them from an Orthodox cemetery on both sides of the winding road. Nobody from the truck had time to return fire, to shoot even one single bullet; in a second they were scorched by the scalding heat of lead. The first soldiers who came to the rescue, hoping that at least a few had held out resisting, did not find their corpses. It was the biggest loss that the Srebrenica forces ever suffered. After an exchange took place a month later, their corpses arrived, disfigured and beheaded, so that their families could recognise them only by their uniforms.

During the winter of 1993, the Serbs tried to retake the village. They once even briefly succeeded, but until demilitarisation Zalazje remained part of the ever shrinking enclave. That village held the key to the town. After demilitarisation, Canadian forces set up an observation post on the former demarcation line and stayed there until they left in the winter of 1994. The Dutch battalion left the spot soon after their arrival, although they were about five times more numerous and better equipped than the Canadian contingent.

After less than half a year, Serb soldiers entered the empty Bosnian trenches, thus taking – during an apparent peace and alongside cold and disinterested Dutch soldiers – something that they had not been able to take during the war.

It was already the sixth month of the siege: we were at the edge of our endurance, pushing back limits that the day before we had considered as final. We woke up miserable, in cold rooms with window-panes made out of plastic bags in windows covered by split logs protecting us against shell shrapnel. We woke up exhausted and lice-ridden, without the desire and most often without even the strength to move, without families, alone and abandoned, humiliated, our past violated and our future slaughtered, our present defeated and defeating. And something snapped.

In the past months we had been surviving by leaving the enclave to gather food, secretly visiting burnt out villages and fields trodden flat. Something snapped and, without a word having been exchanged, the decision to put an end to it could be felt in the air. People died like thieves, carrying sacks of wheat on their thin backs. There was something so demeaning in such a death: first they were made into the worst kind of thieves, those that steal from farms, and then they were killed.

Death caused by a shell was quick, painless: the body was torn to pieces in an instant, skin ripped, bones broken. But they lay on forest paths for hours, bleeding, writhing, before they gasped their life away.

In a strictly military sense, the enclave was still far weaker, it had much less weaponry. But in those winter months it acquired a completely new weapon, a weapon nobody apart from us knew about: wrath. After everything that had happened this began to surge up, demolishing the dams of scruple and morality, the first two things to perish in war, the first two characteristics that a victim loses or gets rid of, because they stand between the victim and his survival.

The enclave started expanding like an ink stain, according to its own logic and rules. There was no sense or plan to it, events overtook us and became bigger than the protagonists themselves. Because of or despite that, in the battles that took place from December 1992 to February 1993 the Serb soldiers had no chance of winning. For the first time, their adversaries were people who considered their own lives less important than the lives of others.

I do not know if among the soldiers from Srebrenica there were any, and if so how many, of those people so typical for every war, loners without anyone left on this earth who went to sleep and got up wishing they too could leave it soon; who killed coldly, calculatedly, collecting debts and making sure every penny was repaid.

But I know for a fact that there were many others, also typical, fathers and husbands, normal people who understood that they could not escape and had nowhere to escape to either. People who could not expose their children to the humiliation of watching their parents cry and pack their bags to go to an unfamiliar place, not knowing exactly where, but certain that they would not be welcome. They were fighting to feed their families, saying to themselves and to others: 'So what if I die?' They went into battle with an axe or a pitchfork, without even having been called up.

If the former kind did exist, then their internal rage must by then have hardened, turned into stone, and they must have turned into stone with it. The latter kind were loud, their war cries were addressed more to themselves than to their enemies. There were also some dropouts among them, guys whom war had thrown off the rails of the invisible lives they were leading before the war. They used their weapons to compensate for all the missed opportunities. But war was imposed on all of them – the first, the second and the third category of people – and they behaved accordingly.

It was the strangest army that has ever existed, and the variety of uniforms, emblems and badges best illustrated how it came into existence.

The winter started early that year and was crueller than ever before or since. The cold and the paralysing hunger took a bigger toll than the shells. Cemeteries grew bigger, and when there was no space left in the old ones, new ones were made. Fresh graves were springing up and the forest of wooden gravestones was spreading. We grew used to people dying. People disappeared and we considered it one of the commonplaces of the general horror, impassively receiving the news that somebody we knew, somebody we saw yesterday, had been killed.

Everything revolved around food, of which there had been enough to go round in the villages of the Drina valley. Those villages were now deserted, their pre-war inhabitants either killed in April or May of that year or exiled, many of them to Srebrenica. But one had to be quick and beat the frost that destroyed the unharvested crops.

In mid December, endless masses of people hurried behind the soldiers who were setting off in that direction. Thousands of unarmed volunteers joined them, carrying their ammunition and food. As usual, they did not attack the strongest Serb posts. In order to spare their troops, the enclave forces simply skirted them, cutting off the roads and leaving them half-surrounded. Connections with other places were interrupted and the Serbs were left with just one road, which was actually a way out.

And so it was this time too: the mine in Sase, seemingly an unconquerable stronghold, was bypassed. Soldiers were instead concentrated around the vulnerable undefended road between Bratunac and the mine. One of the two groups that penetrated the Serb positions from behind had the bigger and more important task of preventing a Serb attempt to come to the rescue of the attacked targets. The other group's task was to surprise them by attacking from the direction in which they would be expecting support.

In a town suddenly free of tension, people discussed the imminent battles for a little longer, then a pregnant silence settled. Nobody knew for sure what was going on. From far away behind the hill, a sullen roar of artillery was heard, but there was no news. After three days the guns fell silent, couriers started arriving from the front and the news came in.

The defeated Serb forces had been left with no choice other than to leave Sase, and we were firmly in control of the whole area, nearly up to the entrance of Bratunac. The Serbs did leave, but realising that nobody was coming to their rescue they destroyed everything they could not take with them. The hardest battles were fought on the first day: neither side was used to close combat and the opposing soldiers mingled to such an extent that at times they were in the same house, unaware of the presence of the others.

The place where the ambush was set up was a typical valley village: the houses in Voljavica were big and strong, densely packed together on both sides of the road. The majority of the soldiers were from there; they knew every shrub, every shortcut between the spacious gardens, every bush on the bank of the small river flowing through the village. The Serb soldiers were attacked from where they least expected it and they stood no chance.

The balance was tipped against them, at least according to what several participants in the battle have told me, by the initial confusion created by Almas H. – one of three professional officers in Srebrenica. Using the radio-set taken off a dead Serb officer during the first Serb attack, he guided the dead Serb officer's men to where they did not stand a chance, realising it was a trick only when it was too late.

He himself perished in a later battle in Skelani, but that story would never get a proper epilogue. He was allegedly still alive, stuck under the ruins of a house that had collapsed during a Serb counter-attack, when the Serbs found and captured him. To this day his parents are going from one humanitarian organisation and committee for missing people to another, trying to find out what really happened to him, but to no avail.

The Serbs tried to get through to Sase on both the second and third day, but they were halted in Voljavica. On the little river dividing the village the soldiers of the hungriest army in the world were entrenched, and they had no intention of letting go. From there all the way to Bratunac there was no Serb defence at all, but the attack was not continued.

The Serb population in Bratunac and the nearby villages was in panic. The bridge on the border with Serbia was congested with people trying to flee in cars, tractors, trucks, or on foot, bringing along as much as they could. The reports on the Serb radio from Pale, which I listened to passionately in those days believing thatI should recognise the defeat in the way they presented the news, were full of terms like: 'Alija's falangists', '*mujahedin*', 'Arabs'. As always in such situations, their version of events was so different as to be unrecognisable.

The Serbs were fleeing and everyone in Srebrenica was happy about it, rejoiced openly and believed that for the first time the Serbs had got what they deserved. We gloated over the news of a massacre of civilians. Even if we did not think it was Serb propaganda, our positions were so different that even crime was defined in a different manner. We preferred to believe those who had participated in the battle, who said that when the village was attacked in the early morning civilians ran out of their houses mingling with our soldiers and civilians. To such an extent, claimed those with whom I spoke, that it was impossible to distinguish between Serb soldiers shooting from houses, Serb civilians running out of them, and our civilians raiding the houses while the shooting was still going on.

But we discussed that just in order to talk about something, without sympathy for the killed, without mercy or empathy in the voice. No matter what, it was a stain on an otherwise irreproachable victory.

It was also a certain sign that we were getting more and more like the Serbs, a sign that we were becoming them – or rather what they wanted us to become. Maybe it had happened earlier than anyone expected, but in those circumstances it was inevitable that the victim would start resembling its butcher. We were not too bothered about that issue back then: there was enough food and we could sleep in peace for the next month.

In January the Srebrenica Command – an umbrella term for several people with different opinions and interests, but with roughly the same number of armed men – decided to attack Kravica. It was the only village left on the road between Srebrenica and Konjević

Polje and Cerska, two towns in another enclave in that part of the country. There was much more food in Cerska than in Srebrenica, and the two enclaves had to be connected somehow. Up until then you had to take forest paths to get from one to the other, but these could not always be used because of numerous ambushes.

Bosnian Serbs, at least those in rural areas, have the habit of leaving a piece of dried meat in front of their houses on Christmas Eve. If the meat freezes during the night the year will be good, if it does not – it will not. There was a terrible frost that morning in Kravica, fingers were getting stuck on gun barrels, but the meat did not freeze.

'Muslim forces from Srebrenica, opening fire with small arms, entered Kravica yesterday', the Serb radio reported. It was an unusually terse piece of news, which summarised pretty correctly what had happened on the [Orthodox] Christmas morning of 7 January 1993. None of the usual incendiary terminology was used, there was no mention of *mujahedin*, 'artillery attacks', nothing from the daily menu of Serb propaganda.

It seemed that the Serb officers really could not grasp that their adversaries were continually applying one and the same pattern, just adapting it to the circumstances. And if they did understand, then they could not find the right response, because trucks sent to the attacked village were again set on fire and the village was overrun much more easily than expected.

Many villagers who had not managed to get out on time hid for hours after the battles for the village were over. They were discovered in the looting that followed and tried to escape, shooting at the drunken soldiers, who hungry as they were had been rapidly felled by plum brandy. One of them threw a hand grenade, killing seven soldiers assembled around a vat of *rakija*.

As they entered other people's houses, cellars and storage rooms, civilians from Srebrenica found desperate owners who knew they could not get away and were that much more dangerous. Both perished there and remained there. They were left to rot and nobody paid attention to the rotting corpses lying along the road and between the houses.

After the attack, women and men from Srebrenica and Cerska returned over several days to Kravica and took everything that could be useful. The village was thoroughly destroyed: all Muslim houses had been plundered or burnt down a while ago, now it was the turn of the Serb ones. Nothing was preserved. They took even completely useless things, ripped cables out of walls, frames out of windows, took tiles off the roofs, loaded wooden rafters onto horse-drawn carts. Left behind were only bare, burnt walls with traces of soot, on which a thin crust of ice had formed. The inhabitants of neighbouring villages at their leisure pulled down even those walls, knocking them down with hammers and patiently cleaning the bricks for hours before taking even them away.

It was the culmination of what the Serbs saw from the beginning not as a loss but as a humiliation. Their self-confidence, or rather their sense of superiority, was smashed into pieces. Exiled from their homes on Christmas, just as we had been eight months earlier on Bajram, they left behind just as we did whole tables groaning with food. The bread was still hot when the first bullets started whistling above the village.

Images from previous months were being repeated: the border crossings to Serbia were jammed with civilians, men who had discarded up their weapons intermingled with women and children, all of them in a headlong flight. A new wave of panic also gripped the shocked town population. Bratunac was deserted. A strange peace had set in. The front was quiet, the Serb artillery had gone silent, and shouting between the trenches ceased. Both sides were waiting. One with fear, the other full of hope. The silence was frightening for one side and soothing for the other. One was thinking of sins and the other of injustices.

Srebrenica briefly moved onto the streets, drawn out by the weak winter sun and the truce. The streets were once again full of people and they all had the same thing on their minds, their glowing eyes turning towards Bratunac. Then and never again I wished I could go home, at that time there was still a chance to patch up what was left of our lives. At the time I was still childishly naive enough to think thatI should finally finish secondary school, enrol in university and catch up with my own life, because, for God's sake, the war could not last long after this.

But this time too, deafened by a babble of general expectation that was little if at all different to my own expectations, I was to be surprised by the war.

It was in an atmosphere like this that at the end of January the impatiently awaited war council, that would normally be held on the eve of any operation, took place. No other before or since attracted such attention. From no other war council was so much expected, none disappointed us more and for no other did we pay such a high price. Since early morning the most curious, and I confess to being among them, had been pacing to and fro in front of the headquarters; it would have been too conspicuous just to stand around there.

Eager to be there and find out the result, I paid no attention to the frost pinching my feet in their cracked shoes, while my body stiffened from cold under my thin jacket. The meeting was obviously difficult and lasted for hours. They came out one after another, smiling with satisfaction or serious and frowning. The last to leave the building was Naser Orić, who quickly got into a car as if he did not want to face questioning looks. From what I managed to find out about the relationships within that disparate group of people, although formally the commander he was actually 'the first among equals' and could not take decisions such as the one they were discussing that morning by himself.

Investigating what had happened at that meeting, I learnt that Orić had found himself in a minority with his request for a general attack on Bratunac, which was completely deserted and undefended. But all the other commanders – especially those from the southern part of the enclave – were against it and simply blackmailed him. They said they would participate only in an attack on the Serb positions south of the enclave. They were not interested in Bratunac. With the liberation of the first town in the Drina valley, right on the Serbian frontier, the course of the war would have been irreversibly changed – and that would have put all their little feuds in danger. As a result, the decision was taken to carry out a joint attack on Skelani.

Skelani was right on the border, some forty kilometres from Srebrenica and separated from Serbia only by a short bridge over the Drina. The place was important also because of the hydroelectric power plant in Bajina Bašta, just opposite on the right bank of the Drina.

In late 1992 several Bosnian soldiers had managed to get through to the bridge in order to blow it up, naively believing that this would at least briefly stop the support the Serbs were receiving via the bridge. But the guards on the bridge discovered them before they could set the explosives. Jumping into the cold river, they escaped being captured by a whisker. Since then, both sides behaved as if they were happy with what they had. The Serbs continued shelling villages in the southern part of the enclave at regular intervals, increasing over time the frequency and precision of their attacks, but things generally did not go any further than that.

As could have been expected, the attack on Skelani ended in catastrophe. It was the first military setback and the moment that marked a turning-point. Accidentally or intentionally several shells fell on the Serbian bank of the river and that was a cue, admittedly an unnecessary one, for the Yugoslav army to cross the border. Tanks on the power-plant dam fired at the hillsides above Skelani, thoroughly and precisely demolishing one by one the houses in which the Bosnian soldiers were hiding.

Unable to remain in the narrow river valley, they retreated sooner than planned with heavy losses, leaving behind their injured and dead comrades. The fighting lasted until nightfall, under the protection of which the attackers withdrew.

The next morning the Serbs in Skelani thoroughly searched the ruins of the day before. From underneath plaster and lime they dragged out corpses and helpless, badly injured soldiers and killed them with a bullet in the back of the head.

At the same time, civilians from Srebrenica left no stone unturned in those villages near Skelani of which the Bosnian forces had managed to keep control after the fighting of the day before. The cartridge cases of fired shells were scattered all around, guns whose breeches the Serbs had taken with them stood useless, buried in deep trenches. Hundreds of Serbian or rather Yugoslav banknotes, with lots of zeros and a two-headed eagle, were scattered in the mud in front of a shop with barred windows.

People arrived continually and immediately set to work; they entered looted houses where many others had already been, then came out shrugging their shoulders and disappointed. Some went on to other villages, while a few remained, hoping to find something all the others had overlooked, or maybe they were simply too tired to go any further.

A fairly large group of soldiers still lay wearily beside the road, their weapons stacked in a pile next to them, waiting for trucks to take them back to town. They were disgusted by the sight: many had lost their best friends the day before and not even had time to mourn them; and paying no attention to that were these people, before their eyes looting this nameless village. Without hope for survival, their comrades were in the hospital overflowing with the injured, but nobody was thinking about them. Resignedly they lay on the wet ground, hoping that the truck would arrive before they lost patience.

What happened in Skelani heralded our end, which was as unacceptable as it was unavoidable. We had obviously at some point lost any sense of the broader meaning of what we were doing; we did not realise that we had become a tumour that had grown dangerously big and consequently needed to be removed. In the following two months the Serbs slowly regained every inch of the territory lost and tightened their grip around the enclave. Soon their winter offensive started, and one after another Cerska and Konjević Polje fell into their hands, as did Kravica and the villages round Skelani. Their forces were coming closer to the town itself.

It seemed that the end had arrived. My neighbour, normally a fearful person, stood at the door hastily dressed and wearing a strange fur hat. He clasped a carbine firmly as he listened to the rumble of shooting pouring over the town; the sound started on the nearby hills, hitting the hills on the other side of the narrow valley and then rebounding until it vanished completely. And then the next wave would follow. I was just over seventeen, sitting in the cellar and reading Machiavelli's *The Prince,* occasionally emerging into the corridor to the front door, in order to peer out without much interest.

The town was being heavily shelled, but I firmly believed I should never have to use the bundle of food and clothes that my granny had prepared against the event that I would have to flee from the Serbs and run for my life through the woods to Tuzla. It was 16 April 1993 and on Pribićevac decisive battles for the town were being fought, this time quite literally.I should find out later that the town was defended that day by a handful of young men, some of whom were barely older than me. They were the only ones remaining of the several thousands that had gathered the night before but fled in all directions when faced with Serb tanks. Srebrenica did not fall that night.

On the next day a medium-sized convoy arrived and forever changed the history of this small town. Several dozen green trucks and white APCs waving Canadian flags were lined up behind each other on the main street of the town. They were at least as interesting to the population as the population was to them. Thousands of people surrounded them and everybody wanted to touch one of the soldiers in baggy uniforms and blue helmets, believing they were saviours.

It was a painfully logical end to the otherwise illogical survival of one of the three Bosnian enclaves.

The end arrived that winter. Once the last Serb attacks had been repelled, the area of the remaining free territory was about 140 km². Serb soldiers were visible to the naked eye on the hills around the town. We would watch them line up, come on and off duty at their posts, and they would sometimes shoot at us regardless of the Blue Helmets, who for the next two years did nothing but write down every breach of the truce in an orderly manner.

Thereafter we could go only a few kilometres outside the town, to the south of the enclave, always making sure to keep a safe distance from the demarcation line, because Serb soldiers often raided across it, capturing people or shooting.

A month earlier Fikret C. had been sitting in his bunker and watching the Serb positions on Zalazje. An explosion resounded and he immediately thought that there was another attack. When he approached the barricade, consisting of a tree knocked down across the road and a couple of well-hidden anti-tank mines, he saw a white APC from which smoke was rising. The second APC in the convoy contained the then UNPROFOR commander, General Philippe Morillon.

Fortunately there were no casualties. The barricade was cleared away and the general was able to continue his journey to town some 10 km further on, leaving the soldiers puzzled by his unexpected arrival. Morillon had been trying to enter the town for several days, but the Serbs had constantly prevented him by lying that the bridge on the main road had been destroyed. Eventually they showed him an alternative route on which nobody was expecting him, and where he had much higher chances of getting killed than of actually getting through the siege.

At the very entrance of the town, thousands of people were sleeping on the streets or crowded into basements between charred walls; under a grey sky fires were burning on which refugees from Cerska were cooking the last remnants of the food they had hastily snatched up before fleeing. That is where a day later a placard appeared, written roughly in red paint on a piece of cardboard and set upright like a traffic sign: *Welcome to the biggest concentration camp in the world.* Morillon met up with the municipal president, his deputy and the chief of staff. He slept on the floor of the post-office building wrapped in a sleeping bag and he communicated with Sarajevo via the normal ham-radio connection. Only he knew how long he was planning on staying in town.

But during these days he made many promises, and we all felt the moment was coming when the grey-haired general would leave the town. At the time that would have meant a death sentence for all of us.

The field telephone in the office of the president of the municipal authority Hamdija Fejzić (a phone network had been set up for the most important institutions in town: hospital, HQ, municipal authorities, police) rang too early that morning for it to bode well. On the line was a postal worker, who in a panic reported that the soldiers of the general's escort had started up the engines of the APCs and were getting ready to leave. The crowd that had slept on the street the night before had already begun curiously gathering around the building.

Fejzić quickly got down to work, organising 'spontaneous' demonstrations aimed at keeping Morillon in town. He called upon people to come and stand in front of the post office, in order to prevent from leaving the small group of people on whose presence, according to our deepest conviction, the fate of the town depended. The general's reaction was unexpected: he climbed on top of the building and raised a blue United Nations flag. The drowsy, tired, dirty and mostly uneducated audience had no idea that history was being made before its eyes.

Morillon later left the town, this time by consent, leaving behind a military escort and a team of UN military observers along with a promise to return to Srebrenica. A couple of weeks later, a Canadian military observer sent to the world one of the most important messages of the whole war: planes from the airfield on the Tara range in Serbia were bombing Srebrenica.

POSTCARDS FROM THE GRAVE

That was not the end of our troubles, and the Serb attacks did not subside. Just one artillery attack on a school playground in Srebrenica killed about a hundred people. Blood dripped from the APCs in which confused and frightened Canadian soldiers took the injured with their shattered limbs to the hospital. Another foreign journalist turned up, a freelancer from Germany who had arrived from Tuzla walking through snowstorms and Serb-controlled woods. He arrived together with Senad Alić, a young man born in Srebrenica whom he had met in Tuzla and who had persuaded him to try and get to the enclave.

On one of the days that followed, Senad was standing in the courtyard of the post-office building looking around him. He was somewhat dressed up, in an irreproachably clean US army uniform with a green beret and Ray Ban sunglasses. Wanting to test his knowledge of English, one of the young men in the crowd that had gathered round the building called him over the barbed wire, stuttering out:

— *'Excuse me, where are you from?'*

— *'From Srebrenica,'* replied Senad coolly.

— *'You're kidding!'* – said his surprised interlocutor, who would himself soon start working for the UN forces in the enclave.

When that last attack too had ceased, and my neighbour had wrapped his unused, clean carbine, all shiny from polishing, in oily cloths and returned it to the cellar, a new chapter in the history of the town started. That chapter would not last long and would be marked by survival. Over the next two years, tens of thousands of people subsisted between the rare and increasingly modest deliveries of humanitarian aid, on the one hand, and black-marketeering with the Ukrainian UN battalion and the Serbs on the other. They survived between the daily danger threatening from the hills and the power struggles within the town, in a stranglehold that offered safety only for a limited period of time.

On a hot summer day in July 2000 we are driving to Srebrenica to attend yet another commemoration, riding on one of the hundreds of buses that are taking there what is left of the destroyed families. I am busy with my work – amid the hundreds of journalists on the lookout for faces for their camera shots and names to put under the quotes to be published in next day's editions – when an encounter with a woman shakes me out of it.

'Well, son, you know how my Juso died, on Baljkovica, and Omer stayed in Potočari, he'd brought his aunt's bags there, he wouldn't have stayed, he'd have gone off with Juso, but whatever happens … Now grandpa and I are living somehow, he's working a bit, he has to … if you only knew how Juso's son has grown, this tall, and the spitting image of him … Almir used to come and see us often before he went to America, he'd hug him and kiss him, you should come too …'

She is tiny, nearly faded away to nothing and invisible in her seat. I am listening to what she is saying and her every word hurts me worse than death. She is the mother of a dead friend, one of the thousands of women whose gaze I cannot bear. I am riveted by her gaze, and it is as if I could see in it the death agonies of the boy with whose team I once used to play football, and with whom I used to swim in the Drina. As the oldest in our group of friends he demanded absolute obedience, and we used to fight until blood was shed. I had known him all my life. He was a little older than I was, and as children we did not really get on.

But during the war Juso Cvrk rapidly changed from being just one of the boys from a numerous family living in the neighbourhood

101

into a hero. Not into an animal, as often happened, but into a real hero, admittedly only to me. When fighting on the front he knew no fear. At home he was the same cheerful boy, scarecely aware of having had to grow up too soon. His spiky blonde hair kept falling into his eyes and he spent a considerable amount of time trying to brush it off his forehead.

But as time went by, the features of his once childlike face hardened, and he became harder himself. At times I feared that he would not recognise me, would not want to recognise me on the street. But he did so without exception. He would halt on the street, visibly tired, his freckled face full of scratches, while from behind his back would protrude the tip of a bazooka with its full load of three shells. Sometimes he would be carrying a rucksack of food on his back. He was supporting a younger brother and helping an elder one, who had got married just before the war, to survive.

Only once during an encounter on the street did he tell me, briefly and in passing: 'Five!' I knew that he was talking about the number of Serb APCs and tanks he had destroyed. 'Destroyed' is a false, statistical term – he had set them on fire, 'crushed' them, 'smashed' them. I knew him well enough to know that he did not enjoy killing, that he never wanted to imagine the people behind the iron mass. But he was happy every time he saw metal melting when hit by a missile. To him, an APC had its own separate life that needed to be ended in order for tens, possibly hundreds, of people dear to him to continue living. So he did not hesitate to pull the trigger.

He spent the whole war, or rather the time until April 1993 when he had to surrender his arms, in a group of young men of his own age or slightly older than him. At the beginning of the war they refused to leave the villages around Srebrenica for weeks, and though badly equipped they maintained the illusion of resistance to the Serb forces. Carried out where least expected, their operations, small and unimportant as they were, still managed to sow confusion among the Serb troops. They actually maintained the hope among the enclave population that it was possible to keep a kind of human dignity even under such circumstances. They were not waging a war against the Serbs, but collecting on future debts, fighting in the name of all the future summers on the banks of the river that they would never have, in the name of all the girls they would never kiss, of all the children they would never take for a walk on the main street in town at dusk. But war was leaving its bloody and cruel mark on them too.

As the group grew bigger and deadlier, the Serb soldiers in nearby strongholds could never be sure whether their relief would come, whether they would get food or ammunition supplies that week. Or whether they would once again find a pile of huddled corpses and bloodstained metal lying somewhere on the road. They were getting deadlier, more experienced; they knew what they wanted and how to get it. They were starting a new and different war that increasingly took on the guise of a reminder to our neighbours of yesterday of how badly they had in fact betrayed us. Listening to stories of their raids behind the frontline, I was able to imagine exactly where they had been, whence they had come, through whose garden they had been obliged to pass, as if by passing that way they had wanted to reimprint their shared memories. When I listened or talked about it, more than once I felt a sort of excitement, as though I had myself participated in their undertakings.

Their commander was the first to perish. He was a quiet man, nearly invisible before the war. He was an electrician and in his free time trained one of the local football clubs from the regional league. When the war started, something broke in him too: he was overcome by that dark feeling of injustice. At a time of general confusion, when all the men were hiding in the woods in the hope that this would save their villages from being set on fire, he was among the rare few who were brave enough to take any kind of initiative. I remember the first time I saw him after the war had started: he was in a large group of people who were anxiously sitting in a big meadow on the edge of the forest. I cannot explain why this was, except that people were probably seeking protection in numbers, in a crowd, expecting everything to be over as quickly as it had started.

He suddenly appeared from a nearby clump of trees and said:

'Folks, we've decided to take to the woods – those who want to join us are welcome; those who don't want to, don't have to!' A smallish group of boys was standing behind him.

The last time I saw him was several months later: he was sitting in front of the mosque in Srebrenica, surrounded by people eager to hear news from the front. Every word had to be coaxed out of him. He was speaking softly, without raising his voice and without that enthusiasm so typical of the first months of war. The words were prised out of him, grown-ups were hushing children who wanted to come closer and see the coat of arms with six lilies, recently embroidered and sewn onto his green camouflage shirt. He was holding his rifle as mothers hold children; it was alive in his arms. Just over seven days later he died. According to one of the versions of his death, he got killed after an action in the summer of 1992 while sitting in a meadow, confident that the danger was over. He was shot by one of our own snipers, who thought that the person in the JNA camouflage uniform was in fact a Serb officer.

From then on, and for a reason I did not try to understand, I saw the whole unit including Juso in town increasingly often. I think they had been reassigned to another part of the front, where they spent most of their time, with short breaks in the town that was now closer. I would see them together, sticking to each other as if they had become unfamiliar with urban asphalt and insecure about walking in the streets. After several unsuccessful experiments, the survivors were eventually transferred in mid 1994 to the 'sabotage and reconnaissance squad' of the 28th Division: in the meantime among others Hiko, a young man whose name I never knew though he had grown up in the neighbourhood, a young man with the deepest green eyes I have ever seen, and later also his brother Nurudin whom I suspected had taken up arms because of his brother's death, had perished.

I knew that although the enclave was formally demilitarised, they were training in the forested areas of Srebrenica where the UN patrols did not venture. They would walk through the town without weapons, in more or less military formation, then turn onto an unsurfaced road towards Sućeska. After a couple of kilometres a truck carrying weapons would pick them up and take them to their destination. My last recollection of Juso is connected with an exercise like this.

At the end of April or the beginning of May, they walked past the post office in the early morning hours. A Dutch soldier watched them suspiciously from the entrance. I was standing against the fence, drinking my morning coffee and smoking the first cigarette from the last pack I had. As he walked past me, Juso gesticulated over the fence; he put two fingers to his lips asking for a cigarette. I pulled the packet out of my pocket and without thinking threw it to him over the fence. He just put it in his pocket and laughed. There was so much joy in that smile.

We met two or three days later: 'Are you crazy? I thought there were one or two cigarettes left and it turned out to be a whole packet! We were smoking all day long!' 'Fuck the packet', I replied. I was thinking to myself thatI should have done much more, that I would do anything he asked, really anything for him and the other boys. And I do not know if I should thank God for getting away with so little, so shamelessly little, with just a packet of cigarettes.

Two white APCs stopped next to each other in front of a deserted building with bare grey concrete walls. With a long hiss, the doors on one of them opened and three men stepped out of the vehicle. Nervous soldiers with UN emblems on their helmets received them and took them inside a dark and dusty building. On their way to the entrance, they could see several more APCs in the largish courtyard of the factory for prefabricated concrete. Holding their weapons firmly, Canadian soldiers were sitting on top of them.

After the three had disappeared into the building, the second APC opened and another three men stepped out of it. One had a big grey-haired head and was in his sixties, the second was middle-aged and the third one was strikingly young. Two soldiers, one ahead and the other behind them, took them through the long straight corridors. After several turns in a darkness broken only by the torch of the soldier walking ahead, they entered a square room in which a table had been set up, with plastic tumblers and papers and pens neatly arranged on both sides. On the corner of the table was a pot in which weak American coffee was steaming and on one side of the table three men were already seated.

One of these was Naser Orić, another his chief of staff Ramiz Bećirović, while I, the interpreter, was sitting at the end of the table. The elderly man who in the meantime had taken a seat on the other side was Cvijetin Vuksić, and he introduced himself as commander of the Bratunac brigade of the Republika Srpska army. Next to him sat Momir Nikolić, who introduced himself as the chief of staff, though I later found out he was actually the security officer. It was late summer 1993, and this was the first such meeting between enemies who had briefly had to lay down their arms. The meeting had been organised after some trouble by the commander of the Canadian battalion, who arrived last and took his seat at the head of the table.

Vuksić's interpreter Stanislav had just been picked up from the front, judging by his dirty uniform, his rough hands, the dirt under his fingernails and the smell he gave off. His English was very poor and I could not understand what his role was, if not entirely ornamental. The building in which the meeting was taking place used to be a factory for prefabricated concrete components before the war, and was situated just a couple of hundred metres inside the enclave; so he was not feeling quite safe, despite the extensive security measures undertaken by the UN.

The other two were equally nervous, knowing that the Serbs were very close. The surrounding houses were packed with soldiers who had arrived the night before in case something went wrong. The meeting was supposed to be the first in a series but it soon turned into an argument; accusations flowed from both sides and the Canadian on several occasions had to calm down the excited interlocutors. But the conversation kept returning to the numbers of victims, to crimes against civilians, and the Serb colonel repeatedly declared that: 'the Muslims had killed sixteen members' of his family.

It is irrelevant who actually mentioned the massacre that had occurred at the beginning of March 1993 in Srebrenica. It was an artillery attack on the town during which about a hundred people died because the shells hit a football ground where, during a brief truce, a football tournament was taking place. I do not know what made Vuksić say in front of four witnesses that he had personally ordered the attack.

He did not even stop there. He went on to say that he would do it all over again, that he would issue such an order knowing what the consequences of the attack would be. I was translating under my breath, in order not to disturb his inspired speech, and I watched him speak: he firmly believed that he had done the right thing, he was so convinced that he would have done it again.

I was frozen rigid. In front of me was one of the people I had wondered about and despised hundreds of times over every time a shell exploded, because after all they had killed children, other people's children whom they did not know. I looked at him and for the first time my feelings were mixed: instead of contempt I felt fear, and I despised myself for being scared of him. In front of me was a man who had at least a hundred lives on his conscience, and I could not help feeling only fear, because my instinct was telling me that this time he was on the winning side.

It had been one of the last attacks on the town, but the number of victims had been greater than ever before. Only four shells fell onto the concrete playground in front of the school, in the middle of the crowd. The scars left on the concrete are still there, along with the high white fence full of shrapnel holes. Pieces of glowing hot metal sprayed all over the people, tearing their bodies apart. Death caused by shells always reminded me of how fragile we are, and shrapnel wounds never ceased to horrify me. Four explosions left about a hundred young men dead on the ground, caught as they were running after the ball, and an unknown number of mutilated who were not even admitted to the overcrowded hospital. Some other children play today on that same playground. I cannot help thinking that every time they run out of school to play a game of football, they are kicking the ball over the shadows of people who were dear to me.

One of the things that makes the crime committed in Srebrenica even more horrible is the fact that years after the war everything in town still looked just like in 1995. There was no attempt to conceal the traces of war in the town, the heritage left by Serb shells to today's inhabitants.

When I went there for the first time after the war, in June 1999, I was surprised to discover that there are still a Brotherhood and Unity Square and a Marshal Tito Street in Srebrenica. Maybe the atmosphere would be different, maybe it would be easier to cope with the loss, if those little tin plates bore the names of Draža Mihajlović or Jezdimir Dangić (a Chetnik *vojvoda* from the Second World War). Buildings in the town were still damaged, UN plastic sheets were still on the windows and shrapnel traces still on the walls.

On my way back I realised that a journey to Srebrenica is not a journey through space but through time, a time-leap backwards, a trip to the last enclave of Balkan Nazism. I was thinking that Srebrenica is our 'little' Treblinka, a four-hour ride from Sarajevo and a little less from Tuzla. And at one moment as I was crossing the main town square, engaged in a struggle with the emotions flooding over me, I caught myself tiptoeing. The feeling that I was walking over the corpses of my loved ones was so strong that I could physically feel it.

The traces of shells are still visible everywhere, and those left by shrapnel have been badly and poorly plastered over. Each chipped piece of pavement means that on that very spot someone got killed, too surprised to duck or run to the nearest building. As the war went on we became familiar with the calibres, types and sorts of shells and decided accordingly how to dodge them. This is advice in brief on how to recognise your own death.

Mortar shells used to drive all of us crazy: there was no point in trying to dodge them. Fired into the sky, they travelled in a very high arc, reaching their highest point and then falling attracted by gravity. They could be heard approaching, falling in a straight line, and the sound was such that you thought they would fall right where you were lying riveted to the spot. Thoughts would race through your head as you examined your surroundings, always doubting that you had chosen the best possible shelter – and, of course, everything round you seemed better shelter than the spot where you were lying. The shell was getting closer, and if it were not your life at stake you would bet that this one would get you.

The enclave borders were expanding in the summer of 1992, the demarcation line was moving away from the town, and mortar shells were being replaced by bigger and deadlier calibres. When the first howitzer shell, a big 155-mm one, was fired from a hill whose name was unknown and irrelevant even to those who knew it, there was general shock in the town caused by this completely new experience. It was not only its destructive power, but rather its terrifying speed – the blood-chilling sound that did not arrive gradually but broke instantly somewhere above us.

The bad thing about artillery is that it leaves you no time to think, no time for an internal monologue. Often you would not even have time to duck and the shell would already have exploded with a loud bang. There was less than a second between the moment when its penetrating noise was heard – the almighty 'Zzuuum' – and the explosion. The narrow valley of Srebrenica protected us from tank missiles, which flew over the town; but the artillery shells always managed to 'get in', as if in some morbid contest. They reintroduced us to life, offering us an unwanted opportunity to brush against death. They poured in one after another with a whistling noise and we were not safe anywhere. There was no wall they could not get through, reducing it to a sad pile of bricks and lime. They made us feel so small, so tiny, we barely existed, we barely wanted to exist, until the attack was over and, following a moment of frozen silence, the counting of the dead would start.

Nights were the worst for me. For some reason that I still do not understand, I had trouble at night determining where exactly the shells were coming from. And that was a vital piece of information, because it determined in which part of the houseI should hide and thus whetherI should survive that attack. My younger sister's crying made it harder, and made all of us angrier and more nervous. I have to say that most of the time I did not realise how terrible the things happening to me were. So I used to sit right next to the window – which can be a fatal error – laughing at the rest of the family who were sitting on the floor.

So much for artillery. Multiple rocket launchers [VBR] were an altogether different category. I do not know if armies differentiate in classifying them, but that 282-mm-calibre monster played a special role in my growing up in Srebrenica.

One of the commonplaces of the siege, the VBR drove us crazy with its explosions following one another at regular intervals: boom, boom, boom, boooom. As one poet from Sarajevo wrote, they left 'furrows in the ear'. That is exactly it – they furrowed the ear. The VBR radically shook our previous experiences, opening a new chapter in an unwritten survival manual. You never know which one is the last, you should never try to get up from the ground and run.

After the attack we would frantically search the craters left by the missiles, finding their tails, wings and a perforated metal drum whose use I frankly never understood nor cared to understand. That shit could have killed me. But I guess that holding those pieces in our hands made us forget that they were meant for us all. For a moment they were just normal pieces of metal. Pulling back from our own experience we managed to forget the rockets, which as they rent the air were shining and visible even under the hot summer sun. But we were wrong, thinking that in this way we would suppress the feeling of worthlessness they created in us. That feeling would stay with us for a long time, long enough to give meaning to the moment when we managed to get rid of it. For until then we would ourselves have believed that we were worthless.

***

– 'Daddy, there's no VBR. Did the VBR die?' – the child asked. Lifting a cup of coffee to his lips, the father briefly paused before deciding that it was better for the child to believe that the VBR had indeed died. 'Yes, it died'. We were sitting on one of the squares in Zagreb, I cannot remember exactly which one, just a couple of days after the fall of Srebrenica. Undisturbed, a cheerful unfamiliar world was manifestly carrying on with its life: couples walked on the streets holding hands, a waiter took orders, and a postman brought pensions that day, I am pretty sure. In the middle of it all, a four– or five-year-old boy was sitting next to his father at a table in a café. He had arrived twenty-four hours before from Srebrenica and did not know what had happened. To him, just like to us, the silence was strange, the first nightmarish nights were quiet after all and suddenly nothing disturbed our sleep anymore.

In my eyes that man represented the war. Today he is in custody at the International Tribunal in The Hague, waiting for his trial to start. Unfortunately it is not possible to talk about Srebrenica without mentioning Naser Orić. And vice versa.

Probably only members of his family called him by his real name. When I met him, everybody else more or less close to him called him 'the boss'. It does not really matter whether it was the heritage from his unclear past in Belgrade or whether he got that nickname in the war. I do not think that the nickname relates to anything other than his status in Srebrenica, in which there was no war and yet everyone knew peace was nowhere near.

In the summer of 1994, one of his people entered a warehouse where humanitarian help was stored and, mentioning Orić's name, took a bag of flour, sugar and some other things. The latter found out about it, found the man and beat him up. Later he made him walk through the town with a sign round his neck saying in red letters: 'I am a thief. I stole humanitarian aid'. But nobody knows how many people were actually entitled to enter the warehouse and take whatever they wanted, which was also happening. Orić made sure his name was not connected to that, because he wanted to keep his reputation as an honest hero. But he secretly believed that a few people loyal to him had the right to do it.

In summer 1995 I visited him at his house with a mutual friend. He suggested going riding, and what is more he offered to let us ride his semi-wild horse. I immediately refused. My friend took up the offer, but at one point the horse got out of control, unseated him and dragged him along the ground for several hundred metres.

In a panic he was trying to free his leg from the stirrup, while Orić was running behind the horse, trying to catch the halter and stop it. What remains engraved even deeper in my memory is only indirectly related to this incident. Before my friend had mounted the horse, Orić took it out of the stable and in order to put it in a good mood gave it quite a large lump of sugar. I thought of all those children who had not tasted anything sweet for months – a kilo of sugar cost 15 DM on the black market.

A couple of years after the war, in 1998, I got to read a report by the counter-intelligence service of the Second Corps of the B-H Army, which stated in the minutest detail that he was the very person who had organised the black market. The report was several pages long and listed the names of traders, where and how trade with the Serbs took place, and which articles were most in circulation. And it seems that this did destroy his reputation after all, despite the effort he had put into concealing it.

The first time I saw him was in the summer of 1992. He made quite an impression on me, with his short hair and beard giving him an intriguing aura. He was fit and strong, perfectly built for a camouflage uniform with a 'Delta Force' flash on the left shoulder. He was charismatic, and the group of people who had gathered round him in the town park were gazing at him as if he were a divinity, while he, clearly enjoying this, showed only the vaguest of interest.

I got to know him well much later, after the demilitarisation of the enclave. I even managed to become close to him to a certain extent. He is not someone with whom you would enjoy having a conversation. In fact very few people actually talked to him, it was more a question of him issuing orders. When he did talk, he was aware of his power and did not hesitate to discuss the most private details of someone else's life. His cat-like eyes, almost yellow, stare at the interlocutor as if they want to paralyse him. When I started working as an interpreter I got to meet him more often, but not even then did we talk much. He would come to the post office where the Blue Helmets were stationed to attend the occasional meeting, and after a proverbially brief conversation would rapidly leave the building.

But when I was barely eighteen I involuntarily crossed his path and got to see his other side. I was into my second month of working for the UN, at a time when intensive negotiations were still being held about the borders of the 'safe zone'. Once or twice a week helicopters would land on the football ground bringing officers of the Second Corps, Serb officers, and officers of the UN. They would be transported swiftly into the town and negotiations would start, which would end without any result – as if it mattered.

Still, these visits were important because letters and sometimes parcels with food and money were transported from Tuzla to Srebrenica and vice versa, mostly through Zaim Čivić, then a major and today a colonel in the army of the B-H Federation. Some time in mid June, unaware that another round of negotiations was scheduled for that day, I asked for a day off work. I decided to visit my friend S. who lived in Potočari, but she was not at home. Her mother sent me to her cousin Hamed Efendić who lived in the neighbourhood. Before the war he used to be one of the top cadres of the Srebrenica branch of the SDA, which was literally engaged in a life-and-death struggle with the new town authorities. As I was sitting with them in the garden, I noticed a blue-grey Renault 5 passing by, a car that Orić normally drove, but I paid no attention to it.

I soon set off back to town, and somewhere about halfway I saw a car coming from the opposite direction. When it got close enough for me to recognise the driver, I realised to my horror that it was coming directly at me without slowing down. It was the same Renault that I had seen earlier. The car stopped some twenty centimetres from the front wheel of my bicycle and Orić quickly stepped out.

– 'Are you passing on information to Hamed?' he asked. I did not understand what he was talking about and barely managed to stutter:

– 'What information?'

– 'You think I don't know that he's getting information via Tuzla from Zaim and you just passed it on to him!' he said furiously, his hand resting threateningly on his belt. A gun was sticking out of his T-shirt.

– 'I went to see my girl friend', I managed to stammer, feeling the blood leave my brain and a light mist cover my eyes.

– 'What girlfriend?'

I explained to him that I had taken a day off and that I was not aware of what was going on in town that day, of whether anyone had been there, of what had been said. He was angry and saw me as part of some conspiracy against him, openly telling me I was 'dead' if he was proved right. Only then did one of his bodyguards, who used to be my neighbour before the war, step out of the car and say: 'Let the boy go, I know him, what's wrong with you?' He managed to get him back into the car. Whether that was a good cop/bad cop strategy, I do not know till this very day, but his threatening gaze followed me home. As if from a tape, every single detail of our conversation was replayed in my mind, and I was scared to death.

Only the next day did I realise that I had got involved in something serious. In the early morning I was called to the top floor of the post-office building, where the telephone exchange and the communications centre of the 28th Division of the B-H Army were situated. I was received by Orić, his chief of staff the now departed Ramiz Bećirović, the chief of police Hakija Meholjić, and municipal president Fahrudin Salihović. The interrogation lasted for nearly an hour. I had to tell them everything about myself and convince them that I was not interested in their power struggle or any other. They let me go, but I had the feeling that I had become irreversibly marked.

For some obscure reason, after this incident Orić started treating me as one of 'his people' within the UN. But all interpreters were in a way 'his people'. Despite a bad personal experience with him, I respected what he did during the war. He won me over completely with one of his moves, which I found about much later.

When Morillon eventually came back to Srebrenica in triumph, after the Security Council had declared it a 'safe zone', he wanted to meet up once more with Orić. Although the latter hated meetings, he turned up. The meeting lasted a long time. The General talked about the enclave borders, UN resolutions, respecting international law and so forth, and his subordinates were unfolding maps and drawing blue and red lines on them. Naser was bored and at one point, when the General was not looking, he turned to his attractive interpreter, tensed his chest muscles beneath his tight T-shirt, and asked her: 'Can you do this?'

Despite everything one can say about him today, I am certain that he really cared about Srebrenica. As long as he was there he did everything that he thought might be able to save the town. In winter 1994 he even arranged a weapons deal with the Ukrainian battalion in Žepa. Two million DM were needed. The money was already available in Zagreb and someone had to bring it over. A Pakistani major who was serving in Srebrenica that winter was chosen as the middleman. They discussed the means of transferring the money several times, but in the end it did not happen because the Pakistani was suddenly and inexplicably reassigned.

After a helicopter carrying back some of the people who had left Srebrenica with him was shot down near Žepa, Orić insisted on getting an armoured helicopter to return to the town, believing that if he chose to return in an ordinary helicopter he would be killed himself. When Srebrenica fell, and the command of the Second Corps failed to answer his demands to support a breakthrough by attacking Serb positions near Zvornik, Orić and his people, joined by several hundred soldiers mostly from eastern Bosnia, bore the brunt of the action to open a corridor, thanks to which several thousand lives were saved.

BOOK THREE

HOPELESSNESS

It is the only period of time that still seems far more like a dream than like a real memory to me. Humanity had been used up, and the cruelty cultivated in the war as a means of surviving was revealed still more in this temporary hell. The world in which I suddenly found myself had only one rule: nobody was important enough. We had become recipients of humanitarian aid, units requiring a certain amount of calories per day, apathetic and without any needs other than to be fed. Alone, without my mother and sister who were in Tuzla from the time of demilitarisation to the fall of the enclave, I started believing that one is constantly in a state of war. None of us wasted the attention necessary for survival on emotions, on such simple human things as compassion, solidarity and understanding.

Most of our relations with other people were conditioned by what we could get in return and how it would further our common goal, namely getting out of Srebrenica unharmed. At the same time, the friendships forged in that time and under those circumstances are to this day the most precious things in my life. On the other hand, many of my friends did not survive the fall of the enclave and every memory of them still reminds me of the void they left behind in my life.

Until long after the war I refused, just as I believe all of us did, to forge new friendships. We met people because we wanted to talk about what we had been through, about how we had been reduced to nothing, about what Srebrenica looked like and why we are actually so lonely. My encounters with acquaintances from Srebrenica after the war were always somewhat bizarre. When we saw each other in Sarajevo, Tuzla or elsewhere under normal circumstances, our conversations were stilted and somehow laboured, because we generally did not know what to say to each other. But every time I went to Srebrenica, words would start flowing out of me, conversations would continue at the stage of our lives at which they had been interrupted because we had something more important to do.

I do not know why, but I do know that we were destroyed much more as individuals than as a community. We were destroyed in more than one way, scattered, completely lonely wherever we were, not ready for feelings because since the fall of Srebrenica all feelings were somehow half-hearted, almost burdensome. Ever since, I cheat on the new men and women in my life. I cheat on them with the dead. And for some reason only there – among memories, among shadows – do I feel better.

The only post leaving and arriving in the town were messages sent through the Red Cross: open letters that were more like bureaucratic forms and had little space for writing. The number of sentences was determined by dotted lines on one side of the paper, while the other side was designed for both the sender's and the recipient's addresses. Before leaving the town, each letter underwent strict censorship in the local Red Cross office. After this many were unrecognisable, with entire paragraphs so thoroughly crossed out with a black marker pen that nothing beneath was legible. It seemed that there was an index of forbidden words: the same ones were crossed out over and over again. It was a whole little dictionary that in fact reflected the essence of our lives: army, killed, perished, Chetniks, executed, slaughtered, captured, hunger, black market, crimes, prostitution, despair …

No, these words never got past the zeal of the censors: our truth was not a truth for the outside world. By writing such letters, every time we exposed our lives to complete strangers, to people who could decide at their discretion what our parents, relatives, girlfriends or family should find out about us. But that was the only means of communication with the world outside the enclave walls.

I wrote in my ugliest writing, with a childish hope that whoever read the letter before it reached my family would skip the illegible parts, whereas my mother and grandfather who had seen me write my first letters would manage to read them. I know now that it was very stupid, actually more stupid than naïve, but back then I was disappointed by their replies to my letters. I realised that what was illegible, those parts of the letter that were of the greatest importance to me, the censors crossed out just to play safe.

What made their sin even greater in my eyes was the fact that those letters were completely ordinary. The content generally related to the whereabouts of some acquaintance who had left, to questions such as whether someone had survived or whether someone else had sent any news from their exile abroad. It was basically what separated family members can write to each other. But not even that was I allowed to know.

There could be no secrets in those letters. Nothing in Srebrenica was secret, everything was known in the same way that nothing was discussed. But this was just one of many betrayals, one of those that lasted for years, one of those that prolonged our semi-existence until it too had lost its purpose.

Some hundred metres from the camp, behind the petrol station, stood a little house painted white. The old woman who lived there did so alone, and two or three cigarettes were enough to keep her silent. Every night three or at most four Dutch soldiers would come to her garden, accompanied by a pimp. They would sit down at a wobbly wooden table, hidden from curious looks by a tall hedge, and wait for the girl to arrive. In the meantime the pimp negotiated the price: three packets of cigarettes, or in exceptional cases – if the 'client' had a special wish – four packets. At that time, a packet of cigarettes cost between 20 and 30 DM on the market.

The business was generally arranged a day before, over the camp 'wire'. To the inhabitants of the enclave, the long building at the exit of the town remained 'the embroidery factory', even after the Canadian troops had moved into it in April 1993. After they had left, one of the four squads of the Dutch battalion was stationed there. All day long children would be hanging around the main gate, and even at night under the arc lights, regardless of weather and season. Smaller children would beg for sweets, and when their efforts were unsuccessful they would leave for home exhausted. The older boys quickly understood that they could not count on the sympathy of some generous soldier to survive, so they started trading with them.

The real tradesmen did not like hanging round there, fearing the police patrols that dispersed them by insulting and slapping them. So they only arranged their business there, then went to the other side of the camp, which was not visible from the street, where they proceeded with the sale or purchase.

Everything could be sold or purchased. The soldiers mostly sold tinned food, sports clothing, regular army boots and the very popular waterproof *Gore-Tex* footwear, along with dark-blue tracksuits with unit emblems. As in every war, the most sought-after article were cigarettes, in which there was big money: a whole carton of cigarettes cost 20 DM at the military canteen, which equalled the price of one packet on the market, depending on the brand. For the purpose of comparison, the price of a pair of second-hand trainers or boots was 60 DM, the most expensive footwear being *Gore-Tex*, its price reaching an amazing 400 DM.

Transactions did not always go without incident.

A fourteen-year-old boy whom I knew once tried to cheat a soldier whilst buying a ration pack over the fence. As he was counting the money, the soldier realised he had been shortchanged by 5 DM, so he ran out onto the street in a rage, caught the boy, knocked him down with his rifle butt and started kicking him in front of several witnesses. After that the rules of trading were changed: soldiers wanting to trade came to the fence accompanied by colleagues, who would keep their guns trained on the buyers throughout the transaction.

As for the soldiers, they mostly bought *rakija* and girls. In the beginning, girls came to the gate without a middleman and offered their services for a pack of cigarettes. Their English comprised a few sentences: '*Me fuck you!*' or '*Me suck you dick!*' After the soldiers had agreed, the girls would immediately set to work. Both would go to a dark corner, the soldier parting the fence as much as he could and then taking his trousers off. The girl would kneel down and, putting her head through the thick wire from the other side, she would take his member into her mouth. She would get up after five minutes, wiping off her trousers and her mouth, her face sometimes covered in blood from long scratches left by the wire. Soldiers later made a nearly imperceptible gap in the fence, through which the girls would sneak into the camp. The soldiers would open the fence and then carefully put it back: several of them would then have sex with the same girl against a wall, quickly, like animals, one after another.

The girls wanted cash in advance and generally gave it for safekeeping to one of the boys they trusted, letting him watch in exchange as the soldiers took her one after another. Some girls went to observation towers, where it would not attract unnecessary attention; but after one of them was thrown out unconscious, some of them sought 'protection'.

The two pimps, at least the ones I knew, were young men who lived near the camp. They had traded with the Dutch before; they spoke some English and could make sure that the girls got their money. I used to play basketball with one of them before the war, and the other one was a cousin of mine. But it was only after the war that I managed to get out of one of them some of the reasons why they had at one point both ended up in the town gaol.

He told me how he had mostly been in charge of finding a suitable place for the soldiers: first it was the cellar of a building opposite the camp, but that was too exposed. Then he made an agreement with the woman who owned the house next to the petrol station. All the rest was arranged between the soldiers and the girls. Prostitution, like everything else in Srebrenica, was limited to a small group of people. Only a few girls in town prostituted themselves, or at least did not hide what they were doing. The police had no trouble finding them once it was decided that the issue would be dealt with, and their names were an open secret.

I knew one of the girls, who had also been in gaol, because she lived near the post office. She was an ugly, ungainly, fat girl whose pallor had a sick, nearly corpse-like quality to it. She was very loud, and would loudly curse the kids who teased her as she passed by. She sometimes even tried to run after and catch them, though without success. She never managed to give any of them a thrashing, and watching from the post-office entrance I used to feel terribly sorry for her.

In such a fanatically conservative environment, I was probably one of the rare few who did not blame those girls, because I sensed that they had no choice, that they too had become victims of the situation, which was being exploited by the Canadian and Dutch soldiers. Before the war this girl had lived in one of the remotest parts of Srebrenica and been raised to be a housewife for the rest of her life. I doubt that she had ever had the opportunity to leave her village for any substantial period of time before the war. She probably had no choice, but the soldiers who exploited her cruelly, as cruelly as only war can dictate, did have one. However, as always during those years in Srebrenica, the choice they made was the wrong one.

'Power plant' is what we called it and eventually almost everybody owned one. In the days after demilitarisation, electric power was the least of our problems. But it was the first problem to be solved, even before UN troops arrived in the town. One morning a small, improvised power plant appeared on *Crvena Rijeka* [the red river], which flows through the town. It was very simple: a mill wheel, an electric engine and a simple wire, several hundred metres long, connecting it to the house of its owner.

After that they multiplied, not only in the town but also in the villages, where it was even easier to set them up. Every village stream was used and the entire enclave was illuminated again. Of course, the light flickered on and off because the voltage was constantly changing; but it was still better than oily cloths that stank and offered only a weak light.

In the beginning these power plants were a question of need, but they later became status symbols. The ones belonging to the most important people in the town had a proper, regular water intake and big engines, which meant that they could even watch TV and that the light bulbs in their flats did not flicker. But the reception was very poor because of the town's geographic position. During the soccer World Cup that took place in the USA in 1994, football matches became the priority despite the fact that war was raging. Entire groups, composed of men of course, took TVs up to Bojna, a steep hill above the town where the reception was good. They connected them to a small dynamo, generally equipped with a bicycle pedal, and watched football, taking turns to operate the dynamo.

Wires were interlaced all over the town, hanging from every lamp post and every building. Walking through the town had almost become dangerous, especially when it was raining, snowing or the wind was blowing, because sparking bits of wire would fall off. It happened more than once that an unfortunate owner ended up in hospital with broken limbs because he had fallen off a tree or a lamp post as he was trying to mend the connection. The only disco in town also opened some time after demilitarisation, but it did not use a power plant. Its owner, a member of one of the families that ruled the town, used a generator unit that was inaudible inside the disco, but which disturbed the people living in neighbouring buildings until late at night. The entry fee was two cigarettes and a drink cost five Marks. A drink actually meant either humanitarian aid juice, diluted from powder, or plum brandy. And that was all. Everybody went there – local thugs, officers from the divisional command and often the commander himself.

With the opening of the first 'cinemas' in town, power plants acquired a certain social status. Cinemas were in fact rooms, sometimes divided in two, with one or two TVs connected to a VCR. The films were part of the pre-war stock of Srebrenica's video stores, and the price of entrance was two cigarettes or two tobacco leaves. Imitating life, we queued in front of these cinemas, acting as if it were nothing out of the ordinary. We went to the cinema on our own, or with friends and girl friends, just as we probably would have done if there had never been a war. I only once went to one of those cinemas, and with my girl friend I watched *Three Days of the Condor*, I think, or some other film starring Robert Redford in the main role.

I observed the room lit up by the milky white light from the screen, as couples held hands or kissed, and that cinema could have been anywhere in the world. The difference was that outside the walls of this pathetic attempt at escape, there was complete darkness and a raging war.

God alone knows all that was on sale in that market, what pieces of other people's lives were displayed on its concrete stalls. It was our *agora*, the difference being that the slaves themselves gathered on this square, people deprived of all rights. As I am saying this, something has just flashed before my eyes: an ordinary picture, one of the rare ones not to have vanished during the fall of the enclave, a photo with bent edges, broken and dirty from being touched many times. It is now standing against the glass of the china cabinet in the house of one of the thousands of bereaved families. Two men are in the photo, one of them blonde and haggard, the other dark and short, his face in a smile that reveals his widely set teeth. In the background of the photo are the ruins of some burnt down building, and further back the tin-roofed concrete stalls of the market can be made out.

But that photo is not important only because of those two people, both of whom I knew and saw every day, but because of a third man who had sneaked into the picture without asking and secretly taken up position in the corner. In his eyes you can see that he is uninvited and expecting to be told to leave either by the two people in the picture or by the person holding the camera. But he is standing there with his dirty, curly hair, in a jacket made out of a sleeping bag, wearing 'funeral shoes' – bad-quality shoes from humanitarian aid – and soiled dark-blue trousers.

He is standing in the corner and smiling, maybe at his family, certain that they will never see it but as though he can sense that this is the only document, the only proof of his existence. He has not got a name in that picture; he is just a stranger intruding into someone else's picture because he could not afford a 10 DM photo. Those are the people I think about, figures without name and without identity, who will become anonymous numbers. How many were there, how many of them just did not appear one day where they had been the day before, because some others – who would then also vanish – replaced them? They disappeared silently, as silently as they had lived, as if they had simply stopped strolling round the marketplace, their hungry eyes glued to what they could not afford.

Hundreds of men waited impatiently for winter to be over. They sat and waited for spring in darkened rooms, in semi-darkness broken by a petrol lamp, their faces recognisable only if illuminated by the glow of a cigarette when someone drew on it. They were waiting for the first spring sun, for the trees in the woods to grow leaves and become green. They killed time with stories about their past, because those stories were nicer than the present and because they had no future. They spoke about their families who were now somewhere else, far away.

They discussed that 'far away', whether it was collective accommodation in Tuzla or a flat in Nuremberg, dreaming about what they would do first when they got there. They would buy a crate of beer and open a carton of real cigarettes, then drink beer and smoke proper cigarettes, rather than this shit that makes your fingers and hands go yellow and not just your clothes and skin but even your sweat stink of tobacco. They talked and remembered children they had not seen for years. It could have been 1993, 1994 or the beginning of 1995, and they had last seen their families in 1992, some maybe a little later in the spring of 1993.

The children had grown up in the meantime, and their fathers thought that they were growing up too quickly, that they were looking too serious in those pictures which had been taken with the sole purpose of being sent to Srebrenica. They carried those pictures everywhere, showing them to acquaintances, friends and relatives, once they had thoroughly cried themselves out whilst watching their thin, grown-up and thus strangely elongated children, recognising in them their own features. Hundreds of them waited

133

impatiently for winter to be over. In springtime, when everything becomes green, they would get to Tuzla through the woods.

Keeping the day of their departure secret, they would leave at night in groups of five, maximum six. At dawn they would reach the Serb positions and pass through them when the Serb soldiers on guard were drowsy and the rest fast asleep. They thought that crossing the Serb minefields was the biggest obstacle on the road to free territory, picturing the more than one hundred kilometres lying ahead of them as deserted, burnt land that nobody controlled.

It was indeed a large stretch of deserted and burnt land, but it was patrolled by the Serbs. Mines were all over the place, and travellers also had to avoid Serb villagers who might discover them as they mowed their grass or tended their cattle. They took the road that tens of thousands of people would take in July 1995, pursued by the Serbs. They would pass between the Serb trenches on the north of the enclave on Buljim, then head towards Konjević Polje.

They would rest during the day and then at night cross a road that was extremely important, hence well guarded. Next to the road flows the rapid and cold mountain river Jadar, which rises with the spring rains: it too had to be crossed. They would then quickly climb the mountain rising above, so that they could rest in the safety of the woods. The road continued through numerous hills in the vicinity of Zvornik, through burnt out Muslim villages in which they could seek shelter in case of a storm, and through Serb villages that were recognisable by the lights in the houses and the barking of dogs.

Days would pass before they finally got close to the frontline near Tuzla and found a favourable moment to cross the Serb positions and enter no-man's land. That was the most dangerous part of the whole journey: they were within reach of Serb guns; mines were everywhere, laid equally by Serb and by Bosnian soldiers; and the latter would shoot at figures coming from the direction of the Serb positions. No one knows how many people left the town during the three years of the 'safe area', just as no one knows how many of them made it to their destinations. But it is certain that fewer people made it than departed. The Serbs knew about them. They laid mines randomly on the roads, set up ambushes, and laid in wait for them. Many left the enclave but, finding the corpses of those who had left earlier, went back discouraged. Others continued the journey regardless and somehow managed to make it to Tuzla, or rather to the Bosnian positions, where exhausted, hungry and scared they would be given shelter, just as some others would be in July 1995.

The news of those rare successes would arrive in Srebrenica immediately, more quickly than any other news, unleashing countless stories and exciting the imagination even of those who until then had never thought of leaving the town. And then once again tens, maybe hundreds of groups would get ready, would set off carrying meagre provisions for the trip and a rifle on their back or a pistol tucked into their belt. Some would come back, others would perish or get captured, and only a few would manage to reach their destination. They all left imagining how they would arrive in Tuzla, buy a crate of beer and a carton of cigarettes, then drink and smoke real, proper cigarettes and not this shit ... Their arrival heralded the collapse of the town: it was a sign that a world which all this time had been surviving on its own was coming to an end. The people who had the least to lose – only their lives – were the first to leave.

The only newspaper was called *Glas Srebrenice* [Voice of Srebrenica] and came out irregularly, printed on ordinary A4 paper. Each of the twenty copies was an original, typed out on a typewriter. Only one copy had a front page in colour, generally drawn with coloured pencils, whereas all the other duplicated copies had black-and-white front pages.

From this perspective it is hard to claim that the newspaper ever even existed, since the odds are very low that even one copy survived. Three young men ran the paper, in which the texts were typed only on one side, while on the reverse were some forms filled out long before. The municipal authorities actually let them have some paper at a time when even the bureaucracy was struggling to obtain any. Clerks gave them paper randomly picked off a pile: it was already used, but at least one side was blank.

The newspaper did not contain news – we had a radio for that – nor did the number of its readers ever exceed one hundred. It was passed from person to person, in order to be read by those who published it, their families and friends. It was full of all sorts of analyses, with grammatical and spelling mistakes and big words such as 'geopolitical', 'strategic' and 'global', which were used at random, mostly in order to point out how educated and eloquent the author was. Local journalists published their first texts and poems, incomprehensible and hard to read.

Those texts did not mean anything to the majority of the population, so maybe it was better that the newspaper did not leave the circle of those who were directly involved. In any case, thanks to that newspaper a very limited number of people maintained the illusion of some kind of intellectual life. It was an attempt by a group of people, of which I myself was part as a reader – a reader who incidentally was stealing paper from the UNMO office, so that at least one complete edition could be printed – to give sense to the insanity in which we found ourselves.

Unlike the newspaper, which appeared rarely but in continuity throughout the three years of the siege, the town radio started broadcasting only at the end of 1994. Actually it restarted: before the war there had used to be a municipal radio station mainly broadcasting programmes like 'Greetings and Wishes', very popular with both the Serb and the numerous Muslim population. As they were leaving the town, the Serbs allegedly destroyed the radio transmitter or it had been broken, so that the equipment was out of operation and stored in the building of the former *Dom Kulture* [Hall of Culture]. The attempt to restart the radio remained a sadly unsuccessful experiment. It was not possible to broadcast out of the town, or rather any further than the town centre, the park and the market, where powerful speakers had been set up. When only a couple of weeks later the project failed, the speakers were discreetly removed.

Abandoned by its people and isolated from the enemy, the town could receive information only via the unreliable state radio or from rare visitors who never stayed long. These were generally journalists who came for a day or for a couple of hours, enough to film or photograph dirty streets and talk to gloomy people and boring town officials.

The Serbs determined the length of their stay and the journalists respected the deadlines, happier to leave than they had been to arrive. Groups of children would follow them, curious about their equipment, their rucksacks, shouting '*Mister bombon!*' after them – but in vain, just like with all the others. The journalists would come in search of something sensational, which their very arrival in the town in fact was. They would be looking for answers to questions that seemed silly to us, questions we did not ask even of ourselves. They would be annoyed by the constant commotion, checking their watches and allocating their time like old hands. They were very professional, too professional, as if what they saw did not affect them in the least.

And nothing of what they saw did affect them, with some rare exceptions like the elderly, completely grey-haired *Toronto Sun* journalist whose name I cannot recall. We were in one of the collective accommodation centres, in a bus station whose large interior had been divided up with red bricks into smaller rooms, in order to get more space out of it. In one of those bare-walled rooms, a young woman, no older than twenty-five, was sitting and breast-feeding a child. Her other child was playing in the room. Her husband was away and she was alone, sitting on a foam mattress covered with a grey military blanket. She smiled, her free hand shyly covering her completely toothless mouth, and patiently answered the questions. He was asking questions and I was translating, until I noticed that he was not writing down her answers but standing with his arms hanging loose. He was just nodding, observing the room discreetly so that she would not notice. He left shattered, with his shoulders slumped. All the way to the town hall, where the mayor was expecting us, he did not utter a word.

This was in late 1993, shortly before the Canadian contingent left the town. Another journalist, John Pomfret from *The Washington Post*, was with them in the town. He walked around with his head somehow raised higher than anybody else's, attracting attention with the really huge bag he carried slung round his waist. He approached people on the street, pompously asking: '*Do you think the enclave is viable?*' [English in original] – and they looked at him blankly, not understanding what he meant by that.

Pomfret's article, which I read a couple of months later, did not in any way answer the question of whether the enclave was *viable*. On the contrary, his article was related only to his conversation with Naser Orić. 'We had to use cold steel that night' was the sentence from the interview that remains engraved in my memory. It was the beginning of something that frightened me, bringing consequences that I did not completely understand, a sign that the world outside was more interested in him than in Srebrenica. That could mean only one thing: either we were finished, or we had been finished for months without realising it.

My doubts were confirmed in the summer of 1994 when another journalist arrived in the town. He was the last journalist to visit the enclave, trying to sneak in on a convoy with humanitarian aid. The Serbs discovered him during an inspection and held back the whole convoy on the Yellow Bridge, threatening that they would send all the trucks back whence they had come. After several hours of negotiating, he managed to get into the town, mostly thanks to the good relations that the Dutch liaison officers had with the Serbs.

He was allowed to stay only until the convoy had been unloaded, and he immediately asked for an interview with Orić. He left the town that same afternoon with much less fanfare than when he had arrived, and everyone was willing to forget him as an unpleasant incident. This would have happened too, if after a time one of the Dutch soldiers had not brought a copy of his article to one of the regular weekly meetings with the officers of the 28th Division and shown it to Orić.

The article was all about 'Mafia', and referred to Orić as ruling the town like a 'sheriff', driving the only car in town – and not just any car but a black Mercedes ... Most of what was in the article was not wrong, or at least was not a lie, despite the fact that Orić was furious and the Dutch considered the article scandalous. But the chosen theme did not worry any of them. Yet it implied a verdict upon us all. For the routine of our horror had become commonplace. To such an extent that something dreadful had to happen for the world outside the enclave to understand that anything was happening at all.

BOOK FOUR

THE FALL

The one question I should like to ask all the friends I have made since the war is whether they remember where they were on 11 July 1995. I do not dare to, because I am not sure whether I shall always get the answerI should like to hear. I do not dare to, because I know that in the end I shall find myself alone, without anyone. Despite the fact that I believe I have the right to ask for an answer to that question. Not because I am interested in knowing where exactly my friends were at that time, but becauseI should like to make sure that they did not participate in that betrayal. What happened in Srebrenica during those few days in July 1995 is one of the biggest betrayals of humankind.

It was a time when nobody believed us, when soldiers required an order to be human beings, when our lives were worthless. Not worth even a sip of water. The youngest person to survive the scores of executions that took place between 14 and 16 July was only seventeen years old. As he was being taken out of the truck with a group of men, blindfolded and hands bound, they all asked for a sip of water. 'I didn't want to die thirsty,' he said years later in his testimony at one of the Srebrenica massacre trials before the Hague Tribunal. The Serb soldiers opened fire.

At that time I was in the Dutch base in Potočari, where I was working as an interpreter for a team of three UN Military Observers. The betrayal I saw is different from the one that survivors of the massacre saw. They watched humankind sinking to unprecedented depths, they were humiliated and tortured and it was a miracle that they survived. What I saw was a cold, almost bureaucratic indifference, and a betrayal by educated and, by any standards, intelligent people. People who during those days either did not dare or did not want to be human.

My friends and I were sentenced to death. And nobody wanted to do anything about it. Those who did do something are a shining light in this unprecedented darkness. By saving even one single life they stand out, even without having made any particular effort. They simply stayed loyal to their human qualities. The appalling death toll best illustrates how few such people were.

I do not know how to qualify the ten days I spent in Potočari after the fall of the enclave. It is not the words that I lack, but I am still unsure about my feelings, about the nightmarish memories of that time. I shall never have the same perception of events as other people and it will always be difficult for me to remember their exact course. But I shall remember every face I saw there during those days, every grimace, every name, and the fear in their eyes I shall remember as long as I live.

Of all the things that in one way or another changed my life and the lives of people around me, what I remember best is that one day. Maybe because it had started like a normal, humdrum day, without any importance. When we realised the consequences of what had happened it was too late. Bloodily and fatally late.

That morning I left to go to work early, as always when I had spent the night at my grandparents' place. On my way there I slowed down in order to avoid arriving earlier than necessary at the post office, because I could not stand its chillingly cold and permanently dark interior. The building was already in sight, so I slowed down even more, stopping to light a cigarette in order to waste some more time. It was early, but I could hear the humming of the power-generator unit in the yard protected by barbed wire. The street had been completely empty a moment before, but as I approached the white sandbags at the entrance, I heard someone call my name. Turning round I saw a good friend of mine standing alone on an elevation in front of the hospital, waving at me to come over. I went back towards him, not finding it strange that there was nobody anywhere nearby apart from the two of us. I walked the hundred metres to the little bridge near the hospital where he was waiting for me.

– 'Why ever are you up this early?' I asked, more out of politeness than anything else as I greeted him. When he replied with an indeterminate 'No reason', I knew there was something wrong. He was not the kind of man to be doing anything 'for no reason': nothing in his life was a purpose in itself. He was some ten years older than me. At a time when, aged nineteen and having nothing better to do, I had started drinking a dangerously large amount, he had brought me back to life. He had taught me what he knew best – that everything has a purpose. Maybe under different circumstancesI should not have believed it, but back then I was willing to hold on to anything. He now cut my random guessing short, not allowing me to ask him a second time, and this time seriously, what he was doing there.

– 'Have you heard what has happened?'

– 'What?' I asked as I dragged on my cigarette.

– 'Naser has left town!' he said with a sour smile on his face.

I nearly collapsed. I could feel the fear welling up within me, forcing its way to the surface. But I made every effort to stay calm as my brain searched for answers to all my questions.

– 'When?'

– 'This morning. He, Ramiz [Bećirović], Eka [Ekrem Salihović] and about ten others.'

– 'How?'

– 'By helicopter.'

– 'So is this the end?' I asked, speaking more to myself than to him.

He did not say anything, just smiled once more, turned round and left in the direction of the town, up the gently sloping street. I did not stand there much longer, I set off for the post office, walking faster and faster, almost running, as if it would make me feel better inside. 'It's over, it's the end', I was saying out loud, almost sobbing.

I ran into the building past the drowsy guards, who looked at me in surprise. I kept on repeating that it was over, that it was the end. I was cursing, I could not believe that the end had come, but I was sure of it. I could not believe that those three years of suffering would have such a pointless ending. I started kicking the pillar in the hall, my fear had turned to anger, but then one of my colleagues turned up. I pushed him into an empty room and under my breath told him what I had heard earlier, as if the news would sound less horrible if shared with him. But as always in those situations, it did not. I could not get away from that feeling that the end was near.

Orić's flight to Tuzla along with some of the best soldiers of the 28th Division remains controversial. The order issued to him and the others by the former chief of staff of the B-H Army command, Enver Hadžihasanović, exists and has been published several times. It definitely removes all possible doubt about Orić's participation in any of the conspiracy theory scenarios that started circulating back then. One of the reasons for this is the fact that during its return flight, the helicopter in which he was supposed to be travelling was shot down in the vicinity of Žepa, unlike all the others that had previously flown past the Serb anti-aircraft defences unnoticed.

Immediately after the helicopter had been shot down, I had a conversation with the same friend who was the first to tell me about the flight to Tuzla. According to him, the area from which the helicopter was fired on had been completely empty up until then, but overnight the Serb forces had deployed a number of anti-aircraft weapons. When I first saw Bećirević after that, he looked very bad: he could barely walk and was bent over in a strange manner. But he refused his doctor's advice to rest and set to work as much as he could. I felt sorry for that man, because he had suddenly found himself responsible for something that nobody else would want to deal with.

The Serbs found out about it surprisingly quickly: only seven days after he had left for Tuzla, an unusual request was received by the UNMO. Through the Dutch liaison officers Colonel Ljubiša Beara, chief of the security service of the Republika Srpska army, asked to meet Orić. The presence of such high-ranking officers in the vicinity of Srebrenica was already unusual but their request for a meeting was alarming.

Beara is today accused of genocide before the Hague Tribunal and the testimonies of Serb witnesses identify him as a key figure and the man who planned the mass executions that took place after the fall of Srebrenica.

The more or less orderly column in which civilians and soldiers from Srebrenica were making their way to Tuzla fell apart after a couple of days. Wearied by being constantly on the move and by the frequent Serb ambushes, people split up into smaller groups that continued the journey to their common destination independently. One such group got lost after several nights of walking and ended up in a nameless, half burnt-out village in the vicinity of Zvornik. Realising that dawn was breaking and that they could not continue their journey, they decided to wait for nightfall near one of the burnt-out houses in the village, hoping to be safe from the Serbs there.

That afternoon a Serb patrol searching for water chanced to call at the house opposite their hideout. As she brought water to the soldiers, the old woman who lived in the house asked: 'Hey, kids, are there any Turks about?' As the story has it they replied in the affirmative, whereupon the woman said: 'That's good, I need some food for my pigs!' So the soldiers just laughed and went on their way.

At that time I was in Potočari in the Dutch military camp, totally confused. Everything was happening too fast. In four days a town, its population and its shared pasts had all disappeared.

But the preparations for what was going on before the eyes of thousands of civilians and several hundred Dutch soldiers had taken longer. As early as the end of May or the beginning of June, I came across a report in the office of the Military Observers that had been written a day earlier by one of their patrols on its journey between Srebrenica and Sarajevo. The report mentioned buses with soldiers, artillery, trucks with ammunition, multiple rocket launchers and several SAM-3 anti-aircraft systems deployed near Srebrenica, along the road between Vlasenica and Milići. With a pencil I wrote down the most important things on a piece of paper, including the coordinates of the artillery weapons and especially of the SAMs, which I thought were especially important.

I went up to the first floor of the post-office building where there was a small telephone exchange and called a friend of mine who was in the Command of the 28th Division. Still disturbed by the shocking information I had discovered, I told him what I had seen and we agreed to meet up in the town, near the market. I handed him the paper and we then went together to the HQ, where an intelligence officer was waiting for us. As I was telling him the story all over again, he looked up the co-ordinates on a map and wrote them down.

I went back to work and he assured me that he would encode it and send it all to Tuzla. A couple of days later, at one of the regular meetings between officers of the B-H Army and the Military Observers, he expressed his concern about movements of Serb troops near the enclave, saying that 'according to our sources, movements of Serb troops were spotted here and here,' pointing to the whereabouts of the weapons on a map.

Admittedly, back then I did not know that two weeks earlier a patrol of the 28th Division had spotted unusual movements on Veliki Žep, a mountain close to another enclave, Žepa. It later turned out that Ratko Mladić himself had been in one of the three Gazelle helicopters they had seen. Six modern BMP-80 APCs, equipped with *Maljutka* rocket launchers and anti-aircraft guns, had belonged to the guard regiment of the Republika Srpska army which was in charge of his security that day.

That report too was passed on to the command of the Second Corps of the B-H Army. Both reports suggested that the Serbs were making serious preparations for an attack on the enclave, and they probably both ended up in the depths of some safe or drawer.

This presumption is supported by a message that Naser Orić sent from Tuzla on his own initiative, a couple of days before the attack on Srebrenica. It read: 'Watch out ... Something big is cooking. Guard all routes suitable for tanks from the direction of Zeleni Jadar and Yellow Bridge. This thing is serious, but we've been through worse.' But by then, everything was already decided.

The Serbs were in Zeleni Jadar, food reserves were running low, at least according to the municipal officials, and UNPROFOR did the only thing they knew how to do: they negotiated. In Orić's absence, everything was in the hands of his chief of staff Ramiz Bećirović (who was to die a couple of years after the war irreversibly crushed by what had ensued, never again the same person]. He was still recovering from the injuries he had received when the Serbs shot down over Žepa the helicopter carrying him and a group of officers back from Tuzla.

Ramiz was not the right man for crisis situations: he was careful, sometimes even hesitant; he did not like improvising or taking important decisions. He was economical with troops and resources. His role consisted of counterbalancing Orić's impetuosity. Apart from him, there was not a single army officer left in Srebrenica who by virtue of his military experience, education and leadership qualities could cope with the circumstances. On top of that, the Second Corps did not permit the use of force to regain Zeleni Jadar. When the last Serb attack started on 7 July, everything was in place for a catastrophe.

On the very first day, the defence lines in the southern part of the enclave were lost. There were no reserve lines and the defence was weak. Divisional HQ moved to the floor of the post-office building where the communications centre was. I happened to be there when a courier arrived to ask for hand grenades, of which there were none. He was dirty, tired and kept repeating as if in a trance: 'If only we had grenades, we'd destroy them all. We've got grenade launchers, but that's no good.' Several members of staff took hand grenades off their belts and handed them over to him. But these were not enough. The inhabitants of several nearby villages had already started arriving in Srebrenica, carrying bundles of food and clothes. Infantry battles could already be heard being fought at the very entrance of the town.

The commander of the 282nd Brigade, which was in charge of that zone, begged: 'We're surrounded, we need help!' 'Hold on a bit longer, help is coming', Ramiz was saying from the communications centre. 'I don't know how long we'll manage, they're shooting from all sides.' 'Hold on just a little bit more, the intervention squad is coming!' Suddenly there was nobody at the other end of the line.

On the next day too, the most violent battles were being fought near the southern entrances to the town. Now it was the turn of the inhabitants of the suburbs to leave their houses – the Serbs were too close. The post-office building was teeming: couriers arrived and left, HQ was working on a counter-attack, and the Dutch officers were asking the authorities to take back the weapons they had surrendered in 1993. Their request was refused for two reasons. First, the weapons that the B-H Army had surrendered during the demilitarisation were mostly useless or broken. There was no ammunition for the artillery weapons and tanks anyway, so they were useless as well. Secondly, taking back the weapons from the UN depot would mean that Srebrenica would at least formally cease to be a demilitarised zone, and that the UN would not bear any responsibility for it any more.

On that evening of 9 July, the Military Observers decided to withdraw to the Dutch base in Potočari. The two of us, my colleague Hasan and myself, were supposed to leave with them as interpreters. Hasan did not want to leave, his family was still somewhere in the overcrowded town and he wanted to stay with them. I did leave with them. On our way to Potočari, the Serbs were shooting at us from the surrounding hills. It was only when we arrived at the Dutch camp that I began to realise what was going on. They showed me whereI should sleep. I was talking to one of the Bosnians working for the Blue Helmets. In the middle of the conversation I started shouting, repeating again and again: 'Everything is fucked. Don't you see that it's all over!' He did not believe me.

The next morning I found out that one of the greatest concerns of my boss, the Dutch major Andre de Haan, was the fact that he had left his passport in the post-office building in the town. But a Dutch liaison officer – who later had a drink of *rakija* with

Mladić, along with Karremans – was already there, taking care of his personal things. Answering our question on the situation in Srebrenica, he said that it had calmed down a little, but 'the Muslims had started fighting each other'.

I went crazy. I knew that he was lying and demanded of our team leader that we all go to Srebrenica. He refused. The justification for his decision was the fact that shells were whistling over Potočari on their way to Srebrenica. At each explosion of a 'supplementary charge' – I had had a year of free training – he and two Africans would flee to the bomb shelter. I asked him to let me go on my own.

– *'All right, but on your head be it'*, he said.

– 'No problem. Just give me a map, a Motorola and batteries.'

– 'You know how to read a map?'

– 'Yeah.'

I took what I needed, stuffed my pockets with food and set off. As I was walking to the gate, he informed the Dutch soldiers: 'My interpreter is coming out, let him pass.' The soldier at the exit just looked at me and wished me good luck, sincerely I believe.

I had already planned my trip. I was planning on running from one factory to the next (it is an industrial complex) for as long as possible, then down the river-bed to Soloćuša at the very entrance of the town. There I should be safe from the Serb gunners. I was wearing a military shirt and trousers and knewI should be a target. I jumped over the fence and entered the hallway of 'Feros', a pre-war factory for brake mechanisms. I was amazed to see a married couple calmly collecting mown grass, as if absolutely nothing was happening around them. I jumped over a second fence, then went down to the river-bed.

I did not manage to pass unnoticed. After a couple of metres along the river, there was first a flash and then a sharp sound. Recoilless gun, I was sure. I did not believe that it was shooting at me, thinking that maybe someone else was around. Ten more metres and I knew that I was the target. I walked down the bank and stepped into the river, which was protected by trees. Whoever was behind the gun could not see me anymore, but he still knew that I was there. Several more times on my way to Srebrenica I had to take cover.

Once I was in safety, I re-emerged onto the road. I encountered a young man carrying a rifle over his shoulder. He told me that our forces had carried out a counter-attack that night. 'We destroyed them,' he said, visibly pleased. I never saw him again. I arrived at the post office tired, dirty and wet. Our office had been demolished and everything of any value taken. The food store was empty too. I went to the upper floor full of hope, believing in what I had heard. But I found out there that it was only partially true. B-H Army forces had indeed carried out a counter-attack, but the Serbs had rapidly brought in fresh troops and regained their positions. 'They're here, on Učina Bašča', Nasir Sulejmanović a communications-centre technician told me. He was scared too. Tanks were forcing their way through from Jadar and our anti-tank weaponry was in Potočari, 10 km away. The weaponry was transferred on horseback a couple of hours later, but to no avail: the two men handling the weapons were not able to hit a tank.

It was raining shells on the town and the hospital was constantly taking in more wounded. I went to the hospital and reported via radio what I had seen. As evening approached it was becoming increasingly clear that Srebrenica was falling. I reported that too. In the evening, alarm took hold of the population, which set off for Potočari: the main street in the town was jammed with panic-stricken people trying to get out, to get no matter where, just to leave. Some were already setting off for Bratunac on foot, carrying their baggage.

In front of the post-office building Hasan, in tears, was negotiating with the Observers via a radio I had lent him, to let him take his brother to the base. Later it would not matter, but we both thought then that he was saving his brother's life. I had heard that my grandparents were somewhere in that crowd, and after my attempt to find them failed I left too. The last thing I remember from Srebrenica was a group of men, all armed, standing in front of the post office, tough warriors who had lost all hope. They held their rifles in their hands almost like sticks, and as the sun began to set the outcome was written on their faces.

After some twenty minutes of walking, I turned round and saw behind me a white jeep with three SAS men who had arrived as 'Joint Commission Officers' a couple of months earlier. They had spent the whole day at the front, expecting planes that they were meant to direct. They stopped and I jumped up onto the open-top jeep. The Britons raced along at incredible speed, partly because they knew the Serbs would shoot at us. I tried to contact the Dutch and tell them to open the gate, so that we would not have to stop at the entrance. But no matter how loud I spoke, the wind was louder. Fortunately the Serbs were shooting over us.

At the entrance I was greeted by people whose job I had been doing all day. Laughing, one of them called me 'Christiane Amanpour'. 'Fuck you both' was all I had to say to him. The only thing that came out of Srebrenica that day was my voice. On the basis of what I had reported, and of what he later saw with his own eyes, a fearful but literate military observer from Africa, the Ghanaian major David Tetteh, wrote a report several days later in which everything revolved around one word: genocide. It did not make me feel any better when he asked me to check the report before sending it. Everything that happened in the following days is common knowledge. The planes never arrived and the civilians of Srebrenica sought protection from the Dutch.

On the evening of 11 July I was called to the headquarters of the Dutch battalion. Two Dutch officers had returned from a meeting with Mladić, who had set the ultimatum of speaking to a representative of the local authorities before midnight. My job was to find one of them in the crowd. I laughed: 'Are you insane? They're in the woods now and probably getting ready to set off for Tuzla.' 'Find a school director, a hospital director, anyone!' the Dutch security officer told me.

After less than an hour I did indeed manage to find the director of the secondary school, Nesib Mandžić. When I told him about the request of the Serb general, he just nodded, despite being frightened to death, and followed me to the Dutch camp. I do not know what happened that night, but in the morning I was told that a new meeting with Mladić had been arranged for 10 a.m. But before the meeting had even begun, his soldiers entered Potočari and surrounded the refugees. In the communications centre Mandžić was on the satellite phone, talking or rather screaming at somebody high up in what was then the B-H government. 'But they're already coming in, do you understand, they're already in!' 'The idiot is telling me to ask UNPROFOR for protection', he said as he left, slamming the door.

The Serbs asked to check the camp over, in order to make sure there were no B-H Army troops inside. The Dutch soldiers were ordered to put down their weapons, which they did. When a couple of Serb officers appeared in the big hall where several hundreds of refugees were packed, mud up to their ankles, women started screaming, some even fainted, and children started crying. After the meeting, from which everybody expected a great deal, the Dutch came up with a plan: the UNHCR and the Red Cross would evacuate the refugees under their armed escort.

At that moment, two UNHCR trucks with blankets and food for the refugees were already on their way to Srebrenica. We felt relieved. For two hours. Because that was how long it took for the first Serb trucks and buses to arrive in Potočari. We were once again caught off guard. Petrified, I watched the buses and trucks enter the place. I asked one of the Dutch officers what was going on, far more because I wanted him to reassure me than because I wanted to hear the real answer. With a grin he replied: 'Ratko Mladić is coming to evacuate you lot.'

At the same time, the Dutch colonel was protesting to the Serb general. The following dialogue was taking place: 'Please, I am the commander of the Dutch battalion and I ... ' 'What commander? You're a piece of shit. I'm God here! Translate that for him, translate it!'. The result of the negotiations was that instead of Serb soldiers, Dutch soldiers would organise the evacuation and take the civilians to the vehicles.

In the afternoon I am walking outside the camp with one of the Observers. Fifty metres from the gate is a check-point. 'Who are you?' the soldier asks me. 'I'm the interpreter', I reply and feel my voice shaking. 'Do you have any papers?' I hand him the official yellow card. He takes it, glances at it quickly, hands it over to another soldier, who hands it to a third, and so on until it reaches Mladić, whom only now I see standing surrounded by his officers. He takes a good look at the card, raises his eyes when someone whispers that I am standing opposite him and then beckons with his index finger for me to come over.

My legs are growing heavier with every step, I feel as if I am wading through water and am short of air. When I come close up to him, the world starts spinning round me. Or rather round him, because I am able to concentrate only enough to answer his questions. As if nobody else was around us.

    – 'Hello.'
    – 'Hello.'
    – 'Where are you from?'
    – 'From Bratunac.'
    – 'What are you doing here?'
    – 'Translating.'
    – 'Where are you going?'
    – 'Well … I'm accompanying these military observers, they want to see what's going on.'
    – 'Were you in the army?'
    – 'No.'
    – 'You really weren't?'
    – 'No, honestly, I was under age!'
    – 'All right. You can go to the camp.'
    – 'Can I have my ID card back?'
    – 'Here you are.'

I do not know where that question came from, what gave me the strength to ask for the card, but at that moment I was convinced that this laminated piece of paper would decide between life and death. I had the impression that Mladić was somewhat surprised by that question; he remained silent for a moment before saying: 'Here you are.'

He added something that I have never been able to remember since, but it was along the lines of 'there are a lot of drunks', and that somebody might hurt me if I stopped on the road. As I was putting the card in the back pocket of my trousers, the only thing on my mind was that I did not want to become a nameless corpse. I set off towards the gate, deeply convinced that somebody would shoot me in the back. The tight boots I had borrowed that morning from a Dutch soldier, and which had been hurting my feet up until then, suddenly ceased to be a problem. I had to pass through a squad of Serb soldiers and was expecting to hear a rifle being loaded. They were sitting on both sides of the entrance, their shirts unbuttoned. Some nodded as I walked past fearfully, trying to avoid eye contact. The guard opened the gate and let me in. The 'weights' on my legs were suddenly gone and the joy of being alive was so great that I was ready to take flight.

I survived because Mladić felt like God that day: he had absolute power to decide over life and death. I used to dream about him for months, reliving the encounter all over again and trying to forget the details that were haunting me. I awoke in front of his bloodshot eyes, his bad breath made me feel sick, the stench of alcohol that spread from him remained in my nostrils. I feared that I would go mad trying to explain to myself why he spared me, who was just as insignificant to him as my friends must have been whose execution he ordered. I never found an answer.

A day later (by then I had stopped paying attention to time) nearly all the wounded and medical staff from the Srebrenica hospital were evacuated. Some of them were last seen alive on a UN truck on the road from Potočari to Bratunac. As they were getting ready to leave, I heard the Serbs asking the UN to hand us interpreters over to them, and the UN agreed to their demand. I discussed it with my bosses but they could not offer any guarantee. 'The Serbs just want to make sure that none of you committed war crimes' , they replied laconically.

I was discussing this with a colleague as we watched how those who had been wounded over the past couple of days, for the most part civilians, were getting ready to set off to Tuzla. A Dutch soldier who understood Bosnian came up to me and said: 'Listen, take my gun and wound yourself in the leg, so that we can put you in with the wounded. If you can't shoot, I can do it for you.' I looked at him and then at the *Uzi*. I was not brave enough to do such a thing. That night the Dutch battalion suddenly received a message from headquarters in Tuzla reading: 'The UN is responsible for the safety of two interpreters named Emir Suljagić and Hasan Nuhanović.' The message header showed that it was addressed to Yasushi Akashi, Rupert Smith, and the UNPROFOR commander-in-chief French general Bernard Janvier, and that it came from the UN Forces Command in Tuzla.

I found out later how this came about: fearing for our lives, Hasan had rung up Tuzla and spoken to a retired US colonel, Kenneth Biser, who was at that time working in the UN Civil Affairs Department. He wrote the message and using his connections sent it off to all possible addresses, including as it turned out to the UN Secretariat in New York.

I really do not know how many more days went by before we left Potočari. I remember only the heat of that afternoon of 21 July when we finally got into a car, about ten of us, we were third in the column; the others were in cars belonging to their 'firms', and on the windows were shrapnel-proof blankets that were supposed to protect us from inquisitive looks. As we were crossing the border, I peeped out and saw Mladić and his wretched military salute as the convoy moved across the bridge towards Serbia. I spent that time in a state of semi-consciousness, never quite sure whether all this was just a dream. At night I would wake up and walk around, convinced that I should be left behind if I fell asleep, while during the day the Serbs plundered everything that could be plundered.

I remember an old lady in mourning black, pulling a fridge on a cart under the July sun and stopping every now and then to have a rest, but not giving up on the fridge. I remember the man who used to come every day to take away just one beehive from a nearby meadow. And the one who was loading newly-stacked hay onto his tractor trailer ...

The Serbs had already entered the town as thousands of people poured into Potočari, a small place halfway between Bratunac and Srebrenica where the socialist regime had chosen to build an industrial zone. Some arrived on foot and stopped at the entrance to the Dutch base, others arrived from Srebrenica on white UN trucks. Hanging in clusters, they desperately clung to the trailer or sat on the driver's cabin so that the soldiers behind the wheel had great difficulty driving.

Disembarking from the trucks, which immediately set off for the camp, they gathered in a fairly small area between three factory buildings, looking in deserted halls for shelter from the cold night to come. However, most people remained outside in the open air, lying under broken, rusty buses and trucks, wrapped in blankets. Arriving on the afternoon of 11 July, bringing the news of the fall of the town, in some strange way they were reconciled with the world and with themselves, lulled into the belief that everything would be all right, as early as tomorrow. NATO aeroplanes were rending the skies above them and it was exactly two in the afternoon.

In the meantime, the Dutch soldiers made a side entrance for refugees to enter the camp. They could not enter it through the main gate, because the Serbs could see them from their positions nearby, so they used an opening in the grille-like iron fence, which was out of sight. That afternoon the Dutch had called me in, and one of the officers explained that I should stand there and direct the people as they arrived. I showed them in which direction to go, another few hundred metres straight ahead until they reached a big shed where they would be given further instructions. I do not know how many passed by, possibly five of six hundred women, children and men who did not want to be separated from their families. They all wanted to come in, believing that they were safer than on the other side of the fence where they felt exposed, since the Serbs were shooting from tanks and guns at houses a couple of hundred metres away.

With each explosion, with each pillar of red dust rising from one of the nearby houses, a collective scream would be heard; panic would break out and the crowd would start moving, but only briefly, understanding that it had nowhere to go. It was late afternoon when a soldier from the main entrance asked for my help. Some people, he said, were at the gate and he could not understand what they were saying. I went with him to a barrier some hundred metres distant where a young couple was standing, a man and a girl. As we approached the gate and their shapes became familiar, I wished I could die on the spot. I had been openly in love with her, and we had spent a couple of truly wonderful months together, as far as had been possible in Srebrenica. He was her husband. They stood there, both of them young and frightened; he was only a couple of years older than me. She asked if they could get into the camp.

I looked at them, knowing that no answer would be right, but I gathered enough strength to say what I had been told to say: 'You can come in, but nobody can guarantee your safety. I don't know myself what will happen.' She started sobbing and asked me what they should do. I did not say anything and just kept looking at them. She hugged him. I said I was sorry – they turned round and left. He was killed and several years later she remarried. I saw her a couple of times after the war. She was always smiling, her hair unfailingly curly, and I always wished that I had been able to give her a caress and find some kind words of comfort that afternoon. But it was not a time for kind words.

I walked back to the opening in the fence. There, the same officer told me to go outside the camp and help his soldiers accommodate the arriving refugees. When I got there, I was given a megaphone and ordered by a soldier to tell the people that there was no need for panic, that not everyone could get into the camp, but that they should not be afraid ... Among the hundreds of people who started coming up to me from that moment on, with hundreds of questions to which I had no answer, were my grandparents. My grandfather, who suffered from asthma, was tired and pale from the journey, while my grandmother's face was flushed beneath the several scarves and layers of clothes she was wearing.

I put down the megaphone and told the soldier that they were my grandparents, and that I wanted to take them into the camp. At the side entrance a couple of hundred metres away, which was still open, were standing two other soldiers who let me pass through. I took my grandparents inside the camp, crossing first one big factory shed and then another, where the wounded recently arrived from the town hospital lay on the dirty floor while a big light bulb shone eerily from the wall. I took them to the end of the factory, to a large room full of trodden mud already filled with several hundred civilians. I told them I would be back soon. I never saw my grandfather again. His mortal remains were found in one of the mass graves near Zvornik and brought over to Sarajevo. At that time I was in The Hague as a witness at the Slobodan Milošević trial. I saw my grandmother again only half a year later.

I still did not know how to answer all those numerous questions. I was not able to confirm that they would all be evacuated tomorrow – we were all able to think only of tomorrow – or that nothing would happen to them. I walked through the crowd: one old man whom I did not know looked at me with gratitude, another, equally unknown to me, looked at me with concern – as if they had to propitiate me to feel safe. As if they wanted to entrust me with their lives, just because I was able to talk to the 'almighty' foreign soldiers. And I did not know how to deal with that burden, so I averted my eyes.

I encountered a cousin of mine, he was wearing only slippers. It was clear that he had been caught off guard by the fall of the town, because he was wearing only a thin summer shirt. Red-eyed and tearful, he asked me if he should stay in Potočari or set off to the woods. I do not know why, but without any thinking I told him that he would have more chance of surviving if he left immediately.

He could catch up with a big group that was getting ready five kilometres away on Buljim, a hill above Potočari, to try and get through the Serb positions.

I also saw my imam, and he too wanted me to dispel all his fears with a word. Those who like me grew up in a small, mainly Muslim, Bosnian milieu know what I mean when I say 'my imam'. I started going to *mekteb* before I started going to school, and learnt the Arabic alphabet in parallel with the Latin one. Before me was a man who had taught me my first Koranic verses, taught me to distinguish good from evil, implanted in me my first fears and moral convictions. Now he was sitting in the dust, drawing something with a small stick on the dry ground and shivering with fear. Sulejman *efendi*, as I always called him – I never called him by his last name Hodžić, which at that time I did not even know – had a wife and two children somewhere around, who were waiting for their husband and father to come back. I was looking at him and thinking how long it had taken me to master the 'long a'; how quickly I had learnt the 'Kunut prayer'; how I had once shoved the rubbish from the *mekteb* under the carpet instead of throwing it in the bin, which was my duty that morning, so that I later spent a long time blowing on the palms of my hands, reddened by his cane …

I do not know how I managed to get to sleep that night, but I very well remember dreaming of snakes. I dreamt of big black snakes sliding on the calm surface of a swamp; they were coming closer, skirting water-lily leaves. I was trying to escape, running through the water with my legs sinking into the mud. I was screaming, but no sound came out of my throat. I turned round and saw the biggest snake separate itself from the others and come in my direction, then stop for a moment to glance at me before jumping. I can see its two teeth in its gaping jaws while it is still flying and I know it is flying towards my throat, but I am paralysed; I cannot bend down or duck, I have nowhere to escape, I have reached the end and the snake is already close, a few centimetres away; I am trying to do something to wriggle away, I am once more using all my strength to try to move, I am struggling … and then I wake up. I was awake when the morning arrived in the little room in the building of the

Dutch battalion where we interpreters slept. My four colleagues were lying around the room; one of them was awake like me, while the other three were sleeping the sleep of an exhausted child.

Wide awake, I went outside into the day that would change my life. I could not have known that, nor could anyone else. I spent the next hours waiting, concerned but not too much. Until De Haan ordered me, in true military manner, briefly and brusquely to make a list of the local staff working for the UN. I also had to make a list of the other men in the camp. It was already afternoon when I set to work equipped with a pen and a fair supply of paper.

By then it was already known that the Serbs were separating the women and children from the men; while the women and children were being driven to the free territory, buses with the men were vanishing to Bratunac. The Serb officers who were carefully monitoring the evacuation of the civilians demanded a list of local staff, and the Dutch Command personnel did not want to argue with them. As for the list of other men, I do not know who came up with that idea; I think it was Hasan Nuhanović, because he thought it would be the only way to guarantee their safety. We all thought that once the Dutch handed them over to the Serbs, which had become a certainty, the latter would not dare to kill them if they knew that their names were written down somewhere.

But before I started making the list, my colleague Hasan, De Haan and myself had to do something else, namely to save, or at least try and save, Hasan's brother from being handed over to the Serbs. We were sitting in our new office, a room with bare walls hastily stuffed with communications equipment, discussing what to do. We eventually decided that the best option would be to put him on the list of UN staff as a recently employed cleaner.

There were seventeen names on the list; his name was the eighteenth, the last to be written down on the list. The second, longer list was much more difficult to make. People looked at me in fear as I wrote down their names, dates and places of birth; they wanted an explanation, some refusing to give their names. I replied that I did not know what the purpose of the list was, that the Serbs probably wanted to check whether there were criminals

POSTCARDS FROM THE GRAVE

among them (My God, how much they wanted to believe what I was saying!). Most of them were nodding docilely, clutching at each of my words as if at a straw that would save them ... But at no moment could I tell them that outside they would be received by soldiers who would separate them from their families with a rifle butt; that in a couple of hours they would be on trucks, not knowing where they were being taken; and that they might never see their children again ...

There were 239 of them. Adult, starved, tired, frightened to death, on edge, in need of sleep, grey-haired, thin, bald, dark-skinned, fair... they were cold at night, behind those hollow tin walls; too warm during the day, under that heated iron roof ... 239 there were of them. And they were all killed. The list of their names left Potočari too late, ten days later with a convoy of Dutch soldiers. The Serbs never found out that the list existed, but they would most likely have killed them even if they had known.

Or maybe they would not have killed them. Maybe one of them at the last moment, as they were facing the rifle barrels, would have thought not only of his dearest, of his three-month-old child, but also of that list: 'Hey, you can't do this, my name is on that list!'

Fehim Mašić was my neighbour, a man I had known all my life, and that is probably why I cannot – and to be honest do not want to – forget the look on his face as I was writing down his name. He was holding his newborn baby girl in his arms and firmly holding the hand of his older, four– or five-year-old daughter. They were both looking at me, the child without understanding anything but sensing that something horrible was happening. He did everything that needed to be done, but in his eyes I could read that there was no need to fool ourselves, that he knew he would not survive.

De Haan and I took the lists to a separate building that was once used by the factory management and had now been turned into the headquarters. In a big room, previously a conference hall, the deputy commander Robert Franken was standing, bent over maps that were placed on the table. We took the lists in and put them on the table and he pushed the maps aside. He first took a look at the longer list: it was a succession of names he did not know and the whole thing probably did not make much sense to him.

When he got to the list with our names, he picked it up from the table and carefully examined each name. He slowly got down to the bottom of the page and then suddenly stopped: he stopped at the last name on the page. He raised his hand, that had been uselessly resting on his hip, and pointed his short, fat, round forefinger. 'Who is this?' he asked, raising his eyes from beneath his glasses as though he were a professor and we were bad students who had cheated in order to get good marks in an exam. Almost with one voice we replied that he was our new cleaner.

With a straight face De Haan said that he had been hired two weeks before, but that because of the Serb attack it had not been possible to deal with formalities such as a contract and UN accreditation. 'No, that's not true, he isn't working for you', said Franken and De Haan blushed. He was caught in a lie. He had been obliged to lie in order to save a boy's life.

Franken put the paper back on the table, stretched out his arm to reach a pink marker – I cannot believe he did it with a pink marker, it should have been a black marker – and crossed out a name, a person, a life. Muhamed Nuhanović. He was nineteen and to this day I blame myself, I blame all of us, for putting his name at the bottom of the list. Maybe Franken would not have noticed it had it been somewhere in the middle of the list, concealed amongst our names. Maybe he would be alive if his name had been just two or three centimetres higher up.

He would be alive and I would not remember that sharp stroke of the marker pen, that short pink line beneath which a name showed through, and I would not have this feeling that I have involuntarily participated in someone's death in such an ugly, forced and indirect manner. I left the room with my senses completely numbed by what had just happened a moment before. I walked the few hundred metres to the office, sat at my desk and started typing the final list on a computer, with a feeling that I was irreversibly losing something important. I felt that my whole life was concentrated into that moment when Hasan entered the room and I said, not knowing of another way to tell him: 'Hasan, Franken took your brother off the list!'

Did my words sound cold, did Hasan hear indifference in them, did he feel *my* selfish desire to survive, so that it made him burst out in anger? I wanted to defend myself even though I knew that he was not screaming at me, that he was not threatening me but someone else who was not there. Hasan kept on repeating that he would kill him, that he was insane, and with each new threat he came closer to me. But then I pulled myself together and shouted: 'Hey, it's not me who did it but Franken! Go and talk to him before it's too late!'

The next time I saw him was in the evening, as a long line of people milled in the dusk towards the exit where armed Serb soldiers were waiting for them. Muhamed was sitting on the floor in the corner of what we called the office and Hasan was in the chair, doubled over, his head resting on his lifted knees. Franken had refused all his pleas to leave his brother on the UN staff list. He raised his head and a loud sob broke the heavy silence. Muhamed was sitting motionless. We knew it would soon be time for him to leave. We remained silent and eventually he said: 'I'm going. Whatever happens to the others will happen to me.'

He stood up, deciding to put an end to the torture, and left. Hasan left behind him. Numb, incapable of feeling anything, I stood at the door, watching them as they moved away. I just stared at their backs and saw Hasan hugging his younger brother, until their figures got lost in the semi-darkness of the unlit factory hall, with a big open door at its end.

Just a couple of hours later, we stood in that same hall, seventeen of us lined up next to one another. Walking in front of us, as if before a military formation, was Major Momir Nikolić – he was lying about his rank back then, he was actually a captain – surrounded by Dutch officers, and we stood still, breathless. Nobody knew what the purpose of this formal military inspection was, but we knew that whether or not we would leave the enclave alive was being decided there and then. He came up to each of us, asked a question and laughed, usually without waiting for the answer. His questions related to everyday matters, the answers he himself provided were blasphemously superficial, and he thought they were – witty. When he came up to Hasan, he asked: 'Where's your family?' Hasan replied that they had been taken away: the Dutch had taken his mother, father and brother out of the camp and handed them over to 'your soldiers'.

Both Hasan and I knew Nikolić; we had seen him every week at the regular meetings between him and the Military Observers. He was the security officer of the Bratunac brigade of the Republika Srpska army, and it was he who decided if a convoy could enter the besieged town. His approval was necessary for each drop of petrol for the Dutch APCs, each tin of food for the refugees. I had never seen him react in a human way, but now, in front of everyone, he raised his hand to his forehead and shook his head, saying pointedly that he 'shouldn't have let them leave the camp'. Still shaking his head, he repeated it once more, then returned to the safety of his role as a Serb officer, which he played so irreproachably, and continued coldly questioning the other interpreters.

Ten days later we were in Zagreb, after a two-day trip in the last Dutch convoy to leave Potočari and Srebrenica. There in the UNPROFOR headquarters, we were shocked to find out that the list with 239 names was simply missing. Nobody knew what we were talking about. We cited Franken, who had told us in Potočari that 'he had faxed the list to Zagreb, Geneva and New York and kept the original in his pants'; we cited the Dutch battalion and the civilians in the camp. We were hoping, what is more we were certain, that there was a mistake, an omission – but nothing could be done.

Six fatal months later a UN official dug out the list, misplaced in a pile of forgotten and unnecessary files. The list meant nothing any more to those it had been made for. Their bodies had long since been rotting in gullies, in mass graves on football grounds, and in meadows along the road.

BOOK FIVE

PEOPLE

I wish I could write a story about everyone I knew in Srebrenica. I should like to write an individual story about everyone who was there, whether they survived or not. And in each storyI should like to write that they were, after all, just people, with everything that implies.

I should like to write a story about Vahid Čivić and his wife Hanifa, in whose house my family lived during the first couple of months of the war. A story about how Vahid, wanting to work in a nearby mine, cheated a medical commission and managed to get the job despite his being blind in one eye. He had to read the letters from a white board and, when the moment came for him to read with his left eye, he just used his other hand to cover it, creating a sort of optical illusion. When the work got too difficult for someone in his condition, he submitted a request for early retirement and astounded some other doctors by putting his glass eye on the table.

Yes, andI should also like to write about Senad Alić, a man whose sense of humour I loved, whose courage and ability to overcome our dark reality I admired. I was confused when I found him in his office, the office for interpreters, reading the business section of *The International Herald Tribune* that some Dutch soldier had brought back from leave.

His private library that was full of books about Buddhism also amazed me, even if I doubt that he believed in any of that. When Srebrenica fell, Senad decided to try to reach Tuzla on foot, despite the fact that he could have sought refuge in Potočari. When he reached Tuzla after thirty-eight days of walking through the woods and Serb ambushes, he received a warning from his employer, the UN, explaining that he could not take any more days off that year, since he had already used up all his holiday entitlement.

He died three years later in a car accident near Tuzla. With him in the car was a young man from Srebrenica whose parents did not survive the fall. He was alone and doing his military service; he had come to Tuzla on leave. Senad offered him his friendship, just as he did to me when I had no one in Srebrenica.

Yes, I should like to write many such stories, but I fear it is unfortunately not possible. Instead I have written three stories about four people I knew only slightly. Not because I am afraid of not being able to write about my friends, but because these stories better illustrate what happened to us.

The following two stories were written in March 2002, when the mortal remains of more than six hundred men and boys killed after the fall of Srebrenica were buried in a cemetery in Potočari. There were 600 graves and there will be as many again, even more. I wanted to tell you a story behind those numbers, write that those numbers had families, sisters, brothers, and girlfriends ...

PLC-113, M4, 21, 5 and NK8-074B, M4, 21, 6

At least in my eyes, those two were the soul of that town at a time when it could not be anything but soulless. They were its only voice at a time when all around was deathly silence. Sead and Senad Dautbašić were just as I thought we should all be. Serious, strict with others and even stricter with themselves, they were the most fanatical ham radio operators I have ever met. I saw them every day for more than two years and was greatly amused at how people would confuse them with one another – of course, only after I had myself learnt how to tell them apart.

They were of that rare breed of people whom war could not corrupt: their honesty was terrifying and they had a rare sense of duty. Also rare was the intensity they put into their work. More than once I saw them disgustedly refusing presents brought by peasants seeking to buy a conversation with their family – and that was at a time when every single piece of food was precious.

They were neither of them great talkers, and I had the feeling that they were only able to open up completely to each other. We, the others, were strangers and to us they remained as mysterious as the first time I met them. During the next two years I watched them making plans for bigger and bigger aerials, complaining that certain parts were missing – all of it was unfamiliar to me – and in the summer of 1994 they set to work. I do not know how they managed, but they spent days stringing wires from one hill to another in the narrow Srebrenica valley; they set up metal posts on the roof of the post-office building. In the end, they were disappointed because the signal, or whatever it was, was not as 'strong' as they had expected. And that aerial was definitely the biggest in the country at that moment.

Only thanks to them was I able to communicate with my family during all those years. And I was not the only one. Sead and Senad never asked for anything in return. They patiently waited until the end of the month and their 'salary', when there was one: a couple of kilos of flour and some orange powder, which only started to look like juice once diluted in water. Almost all that time they wore the same faded trousers and shoes from humanitarian aid. They never drank coffee or smoked, but they took every pack of coffee I or Nuhanović ever gave them to Nasir Sulejmanović, our electrician, of whom a mutual friend fondly said that 'together with his soldering iron, he weighed 10kg'.

After the aerial 'fiasco', in one of the side rooms somebody discovered a whole pile of dust-covered Energoinvest computer games, such as *Iris 8*. Also an ancient version of *Tetris*. We all played that game frantically, in which bright yellow shapes spin on a black background at dizzying speed, falling down more quickly than the naked eye can register. The twins – we all considered them as one – quickly became incontestable champions at that strange sport, a sport that was then one of our escapes into some sort of normality.

When the Serbs attacked Srebrenica for the last time, the twins took the radio station from one post-office room to another every day, moving it away from the ones that were exposed to shells. The last time I saw them was in a little room below the stairs where with great difficulty they had managed to set up the radio set. Nihad Ćatić, the only reporter in town, was reading his last report from Srebrenica. Sead and Senad were sitting behind him. I am sure that after Nihad had read the report, either one or the other reached for one of the buttons on the station and said: 'Well, that's done'. And then they looked at each other, happy they had got it done successfully. For the last time.

PLC-40, M5, 16, 19

We were both born in the same year, in the same hospital. We first met in the war, when a fragile peace moved into Srebrenica under the UN's auspices. I had not heard anything about him since 1995 until I saw his name among those of the other 599 killed. The abbreviation PLC stands for Pilica, a village where members of the Bratunac brigade of the Bosnian Serb army killed more than 500 captured people from Srebrenica in one afternoon. I saw him off to his death.

Nehrudin Sulejmanović worked as a medical technician in the town hospital. He was a very handsome and attractive young man, but hidden beneath that surface was a little boy, still ailed by boyhood troubles, who had not had time to grow up. He was secretly in love with a close cousin of mine. Of course, he never told her.

One day, probably in 1994, I saw him leaving the hospital in the early afternoon with a white band tied around his head. He was very fair-skinned as it was, and it made him look even paler. It does not matter how, but as a medical assistant he got himself an appointment with one of the foreign surgeons who came to Srebrenica and he underwent an operation on his ears. He claimed that they looked too big. A couple of us who were his friends were slightly cross with him. We had all heard him talking about it before, but none of us took him seriously until he took us by surprise.

And then all hell broke loose. I still wonder why he actually came to Potočari instead of going to Tuzla on foot. Whatever the reason, Nehro did not do it because he was a coward or scared of anything. As a matter of fact, what he did during those couple of days in Potočari, namely taking care of more than a hundred wounded and helping them eat and drink, took far more courage than anything else. Even more, because from the first day armed Serb soldiers were stationed around the factory.

On the last evening, the day before Nehrudin was leaving for Bratunac with the wounded on a Dutch truck driven by a Dutch doctor, we spent the whole night sitting in one of the suddenly deserted UN containers. Two girls, one of whom he was in love with, and the two of us. I think we were then sharing a feeling of relief at the fact that everything was over, that in no more than a week we would be sitting somewhere in Tuzla. And drinking beer. We talked, I no longer remember what about – but anyway, what would two twenty-year-olds be discussing as the dusk of the whole world was looming? I do not know if we were drinking something, maybe something I had nicked from the Blue Helmets, we were frantically smoking, and the night was wonderful.

I saw him the next day before he got onto the truck. We hugged and promised to buy each other a beer in Tuzla – once he got there as a nurse and I as a UN interpreter. But we never drank that beer. And not because I got from Zagreb to Tuzla six months late.

When I arrived in Potočari in the early morning, I went to his grave first, because it was the most natural thing for me to do. I bent over, knelt down and caressed the smooth surface of the coffin. And I shed tears that were unrecognisable even to me, heavier then ever before. I went back there in the afternoon, but there were four people at the grave, two young men and two girls. One of them was as beautiful as him, she could only have been his sister. All four of them were weeping, but none as hard as she, clutching the grave marker. I stood petrified and at a loss as to what to do: should I go and tell her that I was his friend, that I was the last one to see him alive before his butchers? No, I would not after all. I waited for them to leave and then approached the grave. I leant forward slightly and put my hand on the grave-mound. 'We never drank it,' I whispered, more to myself than to him.

Neretva, a spectacle of Yugoslav cinematography, enabled one ordinary man to enact his own death. Life took him out of anonymity for five minutes and threw him back into it to await his unnatural and violent end.

* * *

Novak's squad has been ordered by Commander Stole to hold back the Chetniks pushing up from the south until other Partisan brigades arrive. After a while, breathless Partisans run in and take up positions behind large *stećci* on a hill offering an ideal view of the field below. As they march, the Chetniks are yelling in joyful mood, singing: 'Make ready, make ready, Chetniks / a great battle lies ahead,' while the Partisans nervously clutch their weapons. The unsuspecting Chetnik cavalry is marching towards the hill. Shooting is heard. The first rows drop in their tracks. The fighting begins. The Chetniks are using rocket launchers. Both Chetniks and Partisans are dying. Žika, then the driver Jordan, then Novak's sister Dana, all get killed; and while Novak is mourning her, he gets killed too. The Chetniks are in control of the hill. Cavalry is riding into the graveyard. One of the Chetniks shoots at Novak's corpse, and another cuts the throat of one of the wounded Partisans. He too dies in agony, as the last among them, with a painful grimace on his face as his blood starts gushing into the dust.

* * *

His name is Nezir Omerović. Nobody knows exactly how he ended up in the film, but among his neighbours from Zalužje near

Bratunac who have survived, several different stories circulate. According to the least realistic one, he had been spotted and chosen by Yul Brynner as he stood in a formation of JNA soldiers from among whom extras were being selected. It is true that Nezir was doing his military service in Jajce at that time, but he only came close to the Hollywood star later on, during the filming. One of his best friends even claims that the little leather bag which the engineer officer Vlado – the role played by Yul Brynner – carries throughout the whole film actually belonged to Nezir. A second, more credible, version is told by his mother, but the story contains large gaps. She remembers that Nezir came back home from the army in the summer of 1963, during the summer harvest. But three months later he was summoned for the filming. Old Mujaga, his grandfather, was angry that his only male descendant was going to do some silly acting. and he refused to say goodbye to him. He simply turned his head as his grandson headed towards the door. But soon after that he told Nezir's wife to write to tell him to come back. Nezir was his rich grandfather's only heir, and the latter owned one of the biggest farms along the Drina. He got married very young, when he was still a child of fifteen, at the wish of his grandfather who thereby thought to keep him bound to the land. When he returned home from the set, he continued his life where he had left it off, nostalgic about his brief moment of fame and tormented that he had never gone a step further. Allegedly he had indeed been offered a part in some film. When he got drunk, he would ask his neighbours and friends, who as in every small place half-mockingly called him 'actor': 'What am I doing here with you? I could have been an actor.' He was reminded of that time by photographs (which later got burnt) with the smiling faces of the then stars of the Yugoslav cinema: Ljubiša Samardžić, Velimir Bata Živojinović, Pavle Vujišić, Milena Dravić.

* * *

On the night of 12 July 1995, a group of people had just started its journey from Srebrenica to Tuzla. During a break, Nezir left two of his sons and went down a hillside to a nearby stream to fetch some water. He never came back. His youngest son, who was the only one to survive, thinks that Nezir got killed there, probably by having his throat cut: the Chetniks would not have dared shoot because the group was so close. The rest of his family (his mother, sister and wife) came every day to the Red Cross office in Tuzla to look through the names of the survivors, for Nezir and his sons Muharem and Nazir. That is where they heard from other women – who were equally desperately looking for any sign and clinging to the tiniest shred of hope – that Nezir had last been seen alive in Kravica, among thousands of captives sitting in the scorching heat with their hands above their heads.

* * *

In his story 'The Other Death', Jorge Luis Borges tells of Pedro Damián, who dreamed about his real, physical death, wanting to change the course of the battle that had brought him isolation and social condemnation. We shall never find out what Nezir dreamed about the night before he died, or what his thoughts were in his last moments. We knew that his celluloid death had to be filmed three or four times, since each time a knife was put to his throat he would laugh. And we know that both times he died as an extra, without taking any active part in two huge massacres, separated by more than half a century, whose only common factor was Nezir himself.

AFTERWORD

BY ED VULLIAMY

After the Massacre, a Homecoming

The snow lies deep, the air is still and seven degrees below zero
– but the shiver is not from cold. It comes from somewhere within
this terrain, from within this building: a disused warehouse on the
country road that runs through the village of Kravica in eastern
Bosnia. Ten years ago this July, 1,200 men and boys were rounded
up, packed into this place and executed, by machine gun fire and
grenades. And Kravica was just one part of what came to be
called the massacre of Srebrenica, a small mountain town nearby.
Some 8,500 Bosniak Muslim men and boys were systematically
slaughtered by Serbian troops and paramilitaries within six days. On
one infamous occasion, cited by Judge Fouad Riad at a trial in The
Hague, an elderly man was skewered to a tree by a knife and made
to eat the innards of his grandson. 'Truly scenes from hell,' said the
judge, 'written on the darkest pages of human history.'

Ten years on, the warehouse at Kravica has changed little. But
for the fact that it was summer then, the shooting, the explosions,
the screaming could have been a moment ago. The walls are pitted
with bullet holes – some now filled with cement, a futile gesture
that conceals nothing.

A little further up the road is the village of Glogova. Here, some houses remain as skeletal ruins, monuments to the killing and burning that began in 1992 as the Serbs attacked and 'ethnically cleansed' the community. Other buildings, however, have been rebuilt – a sign of the remarkable, precarious return of Muslims to the area, to live among the executioners of their relatives and the ghosts of their dead. They have come, despite what befell them here, into a menacing land that is effectively Serbian; some have come back out of defiance, some out of necessity, some to be close to the dead.

Just off the road at Glogova is a field where the bodies of those killed at Kravica were ploughed into the earth. A rusty, abandoned car is the only monument. There are bones beneath much of this terrain, shredded by bulldozers as bodies were unearthed and reburied for concealment. They are still being patiently exhumed, as the immense task continues of matching them with the names of those who disappeared 10 years ago.

The story of the Srebrenica massacre began in 1992. That year, the break-up of Yugoslavia already under way, Bosnia-Herzegovina followed Slovenia and Croatia and voted to become an independent state, in which the Bosniaks (then known as Bosnian Muslims) were the biggest ethnic group. The Bosnian Serbs, however, rejected this independence, wishing to remain aligned to Belgrade and be part of President Slobodan Milošević's vision of an ethnically 'pure' Greater Serbia. They duly formed their own statelet, under 'President' Radovan Karadžić, and their own army, under General Ratko Mladić. And in the spring of 1992, with backing from Serbia proper, the Bosnian Serbs unleashed a hurricane of violence against the Bosniak population that – three and a half bloody years later – effectively achieved its aim with the partition of Bosnia and the creation of the Republika Srpska at the Dayton peace accord of 1995. Some of the first and most terrifying violence was along Bosnia's eastern border with Serbia, which the Serbs wanted to dissolve, along the valley of the river Drina. In some places – Zvornik, Višegrad, Foča – the 'ethnic cleansing' was swift, brutal and effective. Tens of thousands were killed, and hundreds of thousands were forcibly deported or fled into the Srebrenica enclave. For more than three years, a pocket around Srebrenica somehow held out, cut off and surrounded by the Serbian enemy. The town was brimful of its own population and refugees from the surrounding area. They faced a fusillade of artillery fire, day after day. On one morning in 1993, scores were killed when a shell landed in a school playground where they had pitched camp. Somehow, the enclave held on, defended by desperate soldiers of the Bosnian government army supplied by couriers who would bring ammunition on foot through the forests of enemy territory from the Bosnian government-held town of Tuzla.

In March 1993, the French general Philippe Morillon arrived in Srebrenica promising protection by the United Nations; the following month, just as the town was about to fall, it was declared a 'safe area' by the UN Security Council, along with three other surrounded enclaves. Canadian and Dutch UN troops were detailed to protect Srebrenica. But the siege continued, and on 6 July 1995 the Serbs, under the command of General Mladić, who is now wanted for genocide, began a final assault. The international community stood by. Dutch commander Ton Karremans asked for NATO air strikes to halt the assault, but when they came, they were half-hearted and ineffective, too little and too late. On 11 July, Mladic and his troops entered Srebrenica.

Terrified, the people of the town left en masse. Heading north, they split into two groups. Some 20,000, fearing the worst, set off in a great column into the mountain forests, hoping to strike through Serbian territory and reach the safety of Tuzla. Most of the Bosnian army fighters chose this option, leading civilians, children and farm animals along what would become known as the Road of Death. Another 20,000 or so proceeded to the Dutch UN base at the outlying village of Potočari, hoping for protection. They had packed the UN compound by the time Mladić and the Serbs arrived on the morning of Wednesday 12 July. 'Don't be afraid,' pledged Mladić. 'No one will harm you.'

There, in front of the UN force, the Serbs began the separation of men from women and children. The men, they said, were wanted for 'screening'. But the killing as well as torture and rape began right there in Potočari. Women, children and the elderly were taken by bus or truck into territory held by the Bosnian army, to the west. Males, aged 11 to 65, were transported to a network of locations – Karakaj, Bratunac, Kozluk, Branjevo, Grbavci and others – and summarily executed. The Road of Death was meanwhile repeatedly cut and ambushed; thousands were either killed along its route or taken to places such as the warehouse at Kravica for mass execution. By 19 July, some 8,500 were slaughtered, rather more along the Road of Death than from Potočari.

In the years since the massacre, it has emerged that the UN high command in Bosnia had decided the enclaves were a lost cause and, deeming it prudent not to antagonise the Serbs, vetoed serious air strikes that might have averted the massacre. The Serbs themselves began nearly a decade of denial. That November, Karadžić said that 'nothing happened' at Srebrenica, that accounts of a massacre were 'a propaganda trick in the run-up to the negotiations at Dayton'. Other Serbian accounts, including defence testimony at The Hague, proposed that the Muslims had either been killed in combat, fought among themselves, committed mass suicide or been murdered by a despatch of French, Bosnian and other mercenaries in order to discredit the Serbs. They were not believed. In a landmark trial, in August 2001, Mladić's right-hand man at Srebrenica, General Radislav Krstić, was convicted of 'aiding and abetting genocide'. Last year, uniquely among atrocities committed by the Serbs, responsibility for the Srebrenica massacre was finally admitted, at the insistence of the international High Representative in Bosnia, Paddy Ashdown.

In Potočari, where the slaughter began, there is a memorial to those lost, and a cemetery where those whose remains have been found and identified are buried – 1,438 of them so far. The initiative came from the Mothers of Srebrenica, women who lost their menfolk in the massacre. When they first returned to Potočari to claim their site, they were met by hostile crowds, Serbian salutes and spitting. But their project won international backing, and in 2003 the first burials took place. The green gravestones fan out almost as far as the eye can see, and there is space for many more.

Only a handful of men – no more than 15 – survived at the mass execution sites to which the men of Srebrenica were shipped by bus and truck. One of them was Mevludin Orić. He is wan, thin and, in a scrappy flat in Sarajevo, tells his story. When Srebrenica was cut off at the beginning of the war, Mevludin walked to the enclave, through enemy territory from Tuzla, because his wife and newborn daughter were there. During the siege, he served in the Bosnian army as a courier of ammunition from Tuzla. When the town fell, Mevludin was among those who elected to make a way along the Road of Death. But on a hillside near the village of Konjević Polje, 'We were surrounded. None of us had guns, and they took us.' First, Mevludin was bused to Kravica; the warehouse was full, overflowing into 'a field full of prisoners, sitting on the ground with their hands behind their heads'. The bus then went in convoy to the Vuk Karadžić school in Bratunac, site of a massacre of Muslims in 1992. 'Inside the school, we could hear screaming and shooting. They told us to wait on the bus because there was no room. I prayed for dawn to come and for us to move on.' The convoy headed north, and then turned off the main road, 'which is when I suspected that they would kill us all'. At a school in the village of Grbavići, the men were unloaded and packed into the gym. 'It was so hot, people were fainting. They gave us water, but we fought over it so that it spilled, and men were licking it off the floor.'

Then into the gym walked General Mladić himself – 'laughing with his bodyguards' – with news that the men would be taken to a camp. Two prisoners were selected to stand by the door and blindfold the others as they made their way back to the trucks and buses. 'I was on the sixth truck,' says Mevludin, 'with my nephew Haris. We huddled up, so that if we were going to a camp we could be together. They took us to a field, and when they stopped the trucks and said ,Line up!' I knew what was coming. I could see bodies in the field. They were cocking their guns. I took Haris by the hand; he asked, ,Are they going to kill us?' I said no, then they started shooting. Haris was hit. I was holding him, he took the bullet and we both fell. Nothing hit me; I just threw myself on the ground. My nephew shook, and died on top of me.'

Mevludin remained lying, face-down, all day. 'When they finished shooting, they went back to get new groups of men. I could hear crying and pleading, but they kept on shooting. It went on all day.' At one point, Serb soldiers began shooting dead and half-dead men through the head, but still Mevludin was spared. For a while, he lost consciousness. 'When I came round, it was dark, and there was a little rain. My nephew's body was still over me; I could not move my leg, but I removed the blindfold. There was light coming from bulldozers that were already digging the graves. By now, the Chetniks [Serb extremists] were tired and drunk, and still shooting by the light of the bulldozers. They went to those who were wounded and played around with them. ‚Are you alive?' and if the man said, ‚Yes', they would shoot and ask again and again. Finally, they turned off the lights. I started to move a little. I got my nephew off me. I arose and saw a field full of bodies, everywhere, as far as I could see. And I cried, I could not stop myself.'

Amazingly, he says, 'there was another man on his feet. I thought I was dreaming, seeing things. I walked towards him; I had to step on bodies to get to him. I hugged and kissed him – his name was Hurem Suljić.' Mevludin and Suljić walked through the forests to Tuzla, narrowly escaping ambush and death many times. Their journey took eleven days.

Mevludin, now 35, lives for the time being in emergency accommodation in Ilijas, a town near Sarajevo. He survives on a share of his mother's retirement pension, with which he keeps his four children and wife, Hadžira, who suffers from schizophrenia. He spends his days going to the employment office in Ilijas, to be told there is no work.

In a flat in the Sarajevo suburb of Vogošča, surrounded by neighbours also from Srebrenica – invariably women – Sabaheta Fezić, 49, lives with her mother. The mountains remind her of home, where she was once a manager in Srebrenica's zinc mine. Her husband Saban opted for the Road of Death: 'He waved at me as he left – I never saw him again.' Her son Rijad stayed with her. 'He was my only son, and only 17, which is why I took him to Potočari, hoping the Dutch would help us. We were lined up into a column and made to walk past the Dutch to where the Chetnik guards were waiting. They sent men to the right, and women left. They told Rijad to go to the right and me to the left, but I didn't listen to them. I held my son's arm, I said, ,Wherever he goes, I go, too.' They said they just wanted to question him – I said, ,He doesn't know anything – ask me.' Then they lost patience and tried to pull me away. We were struggling, me pulling Rijad on one side, them on the other. He was terrified; his eyes were wide; he burst into tears. Of course, they wrenched him away, and I fell on my knees.' She is inconsolable.

'When I got to Tuzla, I tried to commit suicide, but thank God I did not succeed. I knew the moment they took my son that he was dead, but I went to places where people were coming out of the forest to see if my husband was among them. I wandered the hospitals where the wounded were. Eventually, the last man to see him alive told me he was killed just a few kilometres from free territory, that he had nearly made it. I went back with the Commission on Missing Persons to look for his remains; I found only a piece of his jacket.

'It will be ten years now, but it is like it happened yesterday. My biggest fear is that I shall never find my child. That I shall have no grave, and shall never know how they killed him.'

At the offices of the Mothers of Srebrenica in Sarajevo she has found kindred spirits – some whose husbands' and sons' remains have been identified, others for whom the search continues. 'Our only happiness is to have this place,' says Zumra Sehomirović. 'We give each other the willpower to keep going towards our aim – to find the missing and bury them.'

In Sarajevo, within the Muslim-Croat Federation, the women are in relative safety. For those Bosniaks returning to what is now the Republika Srpska, the future is more uncertain. The return began in a remote mountain village above Srebrenica called Sućeska. To reach it, you take a mountain track and trudge on foot through snowdrifts. There, wearing a hat and a grin, is the man who led this homecoming, Hasib Huseinović.

As Serb troops destroyed Sućeska, Hasib escaped, hiding in a field of corn: 'I saw them burn the village, enter my house and set it alight.' Hasib's wife Tima was deported from Potocari to Tuzla, along with most women from the village, but their son Fadil decided to try the Road of Death. He was captured and last seen being taken to the warehouse at Kravica. Hasib, however, made his own way to the free territory, through the forests for eighty-five days, finally arriving in Tuzla on Tima's birthday.

And in June 2000, he returned to Sućeska. 'When I first came, I was heartbroken to see it,' he says. 'Every house had been destroyed to the foundations. It was all overgrown. Tima did not want to come back, but I was determined to do so. For the first few weeks, we lived in tents, then slowly rebuilt our houses, one by one.' His eyes fill with tears: 'I wanted to be where my son grew up. I wanted to feel a connection to him. I always have this feeling that one day I might see him coming over the hill, that he went somewhere and will return.'

Sućeska, a burned-out shell five years ago, is now a peasant hamlet again, of seven men and thirty women. 'We have returned, but now we need to stay,' says Hasib. 'Our problem is to create work. Otherwise we shall have to leave again. We have all these elderly women here who have lost their husbands and sons. They need machines to cut their grass; they need tractors and help with their livestock.'

Perhaps most remarkable is the return of the Risanović family to the house they watched burn in 1992, in Glogova, where the dead from Kravica were buried. Their home, now rebuilt, is less than 100 metres from the mass grave. Munira Risanović believes that the remains of her brother and her husband Hasan were buried there. 'We were here,' she says, 'when they were exhuming the graves. Just in the field there . . . I am thinking all the time that my husband and brother might be there, right there.'

Hers is a stricken household. Munira's granddaughter Alma, aged one, has a serious eye disease. The extended family lost thirtu-five men in the massacre. 'I wish we could have stayed with the rest of our people in the federation,' says Munira, 'but we had nothing. Here they taunt us with insults, but we have two cows at least.'

The return to Glogova was led by a local businessman, Senad

Avdić. One returnee's car was attacked with gunfire, another was killed when his house was booby-trapped. Fresh graffiti down the road reads 'Knife and wire Srebrenica' – in the massacre, men's hands were tied and their throats cut. 'But we had to come back,' says Avdić, 'if only so that the Serbs failed to achieve their aim.'

Avdić is among those who survived on the Road of Death; he now runs a cafe and mini-market within sight of it. In July, on the tenth anniversary of the massacre, he and others from all over Bosnia and Europe will commemorate the Road of Death, as they walk the route again.

Srebrenica, once beautiful, nestled among forested mountains, is now a baleful, dilapidated town. Buildings are still claw-marked by shellfire and shrapnel; some are skeletons of charred iron. 'It is a shell of a place that does not make sense,' says Emir Suljagić, a former UN translator who survived the massacre. 'A few Serbs, a few Bosniaks, and the entire apparatus behind the genocide still there, intact.' The zinc mine at which Sabaheta Fezić was once a manager has finally reopened, contracted to a Russian firm, but employs only Serbs – Bosniak returnees are regarded as ineligible for work there.

Before the war, the Srebrenica district comprised 36,600 people, of whom 25,000 were Bosniaks and 8,500 were Serbs. Now the population is 10,000, of whom 6,000 are Serbs and 4,000 returnee Muslims, mainly in the surrounding villages, making Srebrenica itself an almost entirely Serb town. In the marketplace, Milan Pavlović lays out his stall of plumbing parts and padlocks. Originally from Sarajevo, Milan left with his fellow Serbs – and their disinterred dead – after the Dayton accord gave the town to the Muslim– Croat Federation. 'We were herded out of Sarajevo like animals,' says Milan, 'to this sad place, where everything is destroyed.'

The present mayor of Srebrenica, Abdurahman Malkić, is, ironically, a Bosniak member of the Muslim SDA party (because the outlying villages have a vote in the municipal elections). But outside his headquarters hangs the flag of the Republika Srpska, and on the door are the crossed Ss standing for the slogan, 'Only unity can save the Serbs.'

A Serb who returned home to Srebrenica after the massacre was Miloš Milovanović. When fighting first broke out in the town in 1992, Milovanović was commander of a paramilitary unit called the Serbian Guard. He now sits on the municipal council for the SDS party, founded by Radovan Karadžić, and is also head of the Bosnian Serb army's war veterans association, trying to secure benefits for those who fought in the siege and 'liberation' – as he calls it – of Srebrenica in 1995.

Surrounded by some of his 'warriors' in a freezing coffee bar, he refers to an ugly incident in early 1993 when Muslim defenders of the town briefly broke through the siege lines and killed Serb civilians as well as soldiers – a crime for which the commander of the defence of Srebrenica is currently on trial at The Hague. It is in this context that Milovanović discusses the events of 1995. 'The massacre is a lie,' he says. 'It is propaganda in order to make a bad picture of the Serbian people. The Muslims are lying, they are manipulating the numbers, they are exaggerating what happened. Far more Serbs died at Srebrenica than Muslims.'

In this climate, it is a dangerous, lonely business for Muslims to return to the town of Srebrenica. Sija Mustafić, aged 72, who lost her husband Mehmed and her son Sead in the massacre, has moved back into town; she puts planks up against her door at night and keeps the police station's number beside her telephone. Her wedding photo, and one of her dead son, adorn the wall of the home she reclaimed from a Serb family three years ago. 'Srebrenica was all Serb then,' she says, 'and the people living here would not let me come and see my own home. I said to them, ,But we were sitting in here drinking coffee together before the war – you know it's mine.' I stayed upstairs for three months, and finally got the court order telling them they had to leave. They took everything when they went, even the telephone lines. But I sold my necklace to buy a few things – dishes and pans. I did it to spite them. I won't let them live in my house. My husband and my brother built it; it's mine and I want to die here.'

As she speaks, a man walks by the window, checking electricity meters. 'He is doing that now,' says Sija, 'but during the war he was burning houses. I know they killed my husband and my son. I know that my neighbours were involved in this. But you can't say this one burned that house and that one killed that man – they were all involved. They wanted me to go to The Hague, but my daughter said people here would kill me, and I didn't. So I don't talk to them. They have their life, I have mine. If I cry, I would die of heartbreak, so I don't. Instead, I fix my house, I eat something, I drink some coffee.'

The dead of Srebrenica were not left to rest in peace. Within weeks of ploughing their victims into mass graves, the Bosnian Serbs embarked on a morbid operation: to unearth and move almost all the bodies to so-called 'secondary' graves, in an effort to conceal the evidence of what they had done from prying international eyes, and especially from The Hague. For months, bulldozers and trucks heaved the decomposing dead from one place to another.

From 1996, however, teams from The Hague began, under heavy military guard, to locate and exhume some of the graves. Their purpose was prosecution: to determine the cause and manner of death, and investigate the guilt of the perpetrators. But they did not try to identify the dead. That is the next task, one of the most extraordinary enterprises in the field of science and human rights: to give every fragmented skeleton of someone killed at Srebrenica a name, to return the remains to the bereaved, and to bury them at Potočari.

Responsibility for the identification and exhumation of mass graves has passed to the Commission for Missing Persons for the Muslim-Croat Federation. Murat Hurtić, who represents the commission in Tuzla, has opened 66 mass graves now, and takes us to the dam at an artificial lake near Petkovci, beneath which hundreds were lined up and shot. We are chased off the premises by the security guard, but follow the trail of the dead, who were dug from here and taken up a winding mountain track to a village called Liplje for reburial. Hurtić strides into the snow: 'In this village, in three graves, are shredded remains of more than 1,000 people. When I came, we found skulls and bones on the surface – they didn't do the job very well. All the graves were in Bosniak villages that had been completely destroyed, to which they thought people would never come back . . . We live strange lives,' he reflects, 'traumatic, but we do it. Because we have to.'

Amor Masović, head of the commission, explains the gruesome nature of their work: 'Each primary grave has four or five secondary graves, so that bodies became split up; there are pieces of the same person spread out across graves all over Bosnia. Therefore we are left with a dilemma: we may only have someone's forearm, and maybe we can find out the name of that forearm, but we don't have the nerve to say to the family, ,We have found your son.' How can you hand over to a mother a son represented by a forearm? But unfortunately death does not wait for us to find the missing. Every day that passes, someone from the enclaves dies before their missing relatives have been found. And that is our moral dilemma: when you find a bone that has a name, do you tell, or do you keep silent? We have talked a lot about this, and have reached a consensus that if 50 % of a body is found, we tell.'

As body parts are assembled, so the process of 're-association' of skeletons begins. At the Podrinje Identification Project in Tuzla, tens of thousands of body bags from all over Bosnia are stored in a tunnel dug into a hillside. Most of those from Srebrenica are kept separately, piled up on shelf after shelf, row after row: white plastic bags for body parts, brown bags for personal effects. From Tuzla, the body bags journey to the centre in Lukavac, where skeletons are reassembled. As we arrive they are piecing together bones originally from Glogova, from the field next to the Risanović family's house; these are the remains of the men who were executed at the warehouse at Kravica.

The third location in the process, back in Tuzla, is the Identification Co– ordination Division. In 1988, the commission began using DNA testing for identification – both from bone to bone, and between bones and blood samples collected from surviving family members. The effect was immediate and dramatic: approaching 2,000 bodies have been identified and given back to their families.

'Having a war crimes tribunal looking at mass graves with a view to prosecution is new,' says Kathryne Bomberger, chief of staff for the International Commission on Missing Persons in Bosnia. 'But having a parallel operation looking at mass graves to try to establish truth – and ultimately justice – in a society that craves it is also a voyage into the unknown. What we are doing is unique in the world.'

And it is unique to Srebrenica. 'There is no collective sense of the atrocities that took place in Bosnia,' says Bomberger. 'And what we are doing is politically charged. The numbers are skewed: 85 % of persons who are missing are Bosniak Muslims, 12 % are Serbs and 3 % are Croats. The numbers speak for themselves; they tell the story of what happened here – but we have to be seen as credible and politically impartial. How do you get people to recognise the horrors? Our work is intended to be a contribution.'

Srebrenica is iconic – the massacre initiated the closing phase of a war that had dragged on for more than three years. The name is synonomous with the wilful inaction of the international community to stop the massacre, and with three years' appeasement of the Serbs. Mladić and Karadžić are now wanted war criminals, but on the eve of the Srebrenica massacre the world's diplomats and political leaders were happy to entertain them. These are the thoughts that haunt Emir Suljagić when he visits Srebrenica from his new home in Sarajevo. Emir survived the massacre – and a meeting with Mladić himself – because he was working throughout the siege as a translator for the UN military observers in the area. He was at Potočari, frantically trying to register names of the men gathered in the factory across the road from the Dutch base. This July, his father, whose remains were found last year, will be buried along with hundreds of others.

Emir has a project – to make a reckoning of what happened at Srebrenica and elsewhere. He has gathered objects found in mass graves – lighters, watches, tobacco boxes, glasses – for a museum to be built within the factory where he took the names that day. He is now tracing the surviving families of the owners of those objects. 'The idea is to make a personal portrait out of each object. When you tell someone that 10,000 people died, they cannot understand or imagine it. What I want to say is that these people were peasants, car mechanics or masons. That they had daughters, mothers, that they leave someone behind; that a lot of people are hurt by this person's death.

'I have given up on this generation of Serbs,' he says. 'I have given up on the people who were my friends, whom I played basketball with. It seems that they will never reckon with what they have done. But what I want is for their children to have a chance to make up their own minds. Children who will be passing by the memorial every day. I want them to know and think about what happened, and to learn from it. And if there are places where the Serbs were murdered, then we should mark them, too. Only then can the next generation grow up and be told by what they see: that this should never happen again.'*

* *A shorter version of this text was published in* Guardian Weekend *on 30 April 2005.*